Charles Johnson's
Spiritual
Imagination

Charles Johnson's Spiritual Imagination

Jonathan Little

University of Missouri Press

Columbia and London

Copyright © 1997 by
The Curators of the University of Missouri
University of Missouri Press, Columbia, Missouri 65201
Printed and bound in the United States of America
All rights reserved

5 4 3 2 1   01 00 99 98 97

Library of Congress Cataloging-in-Publication Data

Little, Jonathan, 1959–
    Charles Johnson's spiritual imagination / Jonathan Little.
        p.   cm.
    Includes bibliographical references and index.
    ISBN 0-8262-1147-X (cloth : alk. paper).—ISBN 0-8262-1151-8
(paper : alk. paper)
    1. Johnson, Charles Richard, 1948–   —Criticism and
interpretation.   2. Civil rights movements in literature.   3. Afro-
Americans in literature.   4. Spiritual life in literature.
I. Title
PS3560.03735Z74   1997
813'.54—dc21   97-33392
                                                                          CIP

∞™ This paper meets the requirements of the American National
Standard for Permanence of Paper for Printed Library Materials,
Z39.48, 1984.

Text Design: Elizabeth K. Young
Cover Design: Stephanie Foley
Typesetter: BOOKCOMP
Printer and binder: Thomson-Shore, Inc.
Typefaces: Viva Regular, Galliard

For permissions see p. 173.

To M. and Q.

Contents

Acknowledgments

This study of Charles Johnson's work grew out of a chapter of my dissertation that analyzes *Oxherding Tale* (among other recent novels) for its treatment of the interracial couple. After reading such an amazing book, I wanted to find out more about its author.

For help with conceptualizing and completing my dissertation, I thank my director, William L. Andrews, and my reader, Nellie Y. McKay, who gave me such expert guidance and support during those most stimulating days of graduate study at the University of Wisconsin–Madison.

To my wife, Maureen, I owe the greatest thanks for this book. Her love of cartoons changed my mind about that medium, and her precise editing of the cartooning chapter made it very strong. Both Maureen and my son, Quentin, gave me the day-to-day tranquillity and joy that made this such a pleasurable project. To Priscilla and David, my parents, I am thankful for their inspiring lifelong commitment to art and scholarship. Their example in many ways made this work possible.

I owe special thanks to Charles Johnson for sending me published and unpublished materials since my interview with him in Seattle in the summer of 1992 and for maintaining a lively interest in my work.

Harry Fleddermann provided friendship and support during these years of writing. I am indebted to Daniel Leister for loaning me invaluable sources on Eastern religions and for discussing them with me. I am very grateful to Dean Kathleen O'Brien and Alverno College for awarding me generous summer grants to study related topics, such as aesthetics and Buddhism. Many thanks to Joyce Lange for her photographic expertise and for her hard work taking the photos of me and of the cartoons. Finally, thanks to Ernest Suarez for his encouragement, even if he did move to D. C.

Abbreviations

The following abbreviations appear parenthetically throughout the text and notes to identify frequently cited works by Charles Johnson.

BR	*Being and Race*
F	*Faith and the Good Thing*
MP	*Middle Passage*
OT	*Oxherding Tale*
SA	*The Sorcerer's Apprentice*

Charles Johnson's Spiritual Imagination

Introduction

The Integrative Impulse

The sleepers are very beautiful as they lie unclothed,
They flow hand in hand over the whole earth from east to west as
they lie unclothed,
The Asiatic and African are hand in hand, the European and
American are hand in hand,
Learn'ed and unlearn'ed are hand in hand, and male and female
are hand in hand.

WALT WHITMAN, "The Sleepers"

In a 1996 newspaper editorial, "Searching for the Dreamer," Charles Johnson outlined his interest in Dr. Martin Luther King Jr., the subject of Johnson's novel *Dreamer*: "I want to know—from the inside—the King who believed in the interrelatedness of all things and the 'inescapable network of mutuality' that binds all people in a 'single garment of destiny.' "[1]

Using King as a fictional subject allows Johnson to explore the Civil Rights movement and the spiritual and philosophical aspects of integrationism. *Dreamer* demonstrates the close affiliation in Johnson's work of the artistic and the political and of the spiritual and the ideological. The novel's central character was formerly sympathetic to black nationalism, but his view changes in accordance with King's more moderate position. In

---

1. Charles Johnson, "Searching for the Dreamer." *Dreamer* is scheduled to be released in fall 1998.

some ways, this development reflects Johnson's own ideological journey, from a political cartoonist immersed in the Black Power movement in the late sixties to a writer whose novel *Middle Passage* (1990) offered a decidedly more moderate message about racial activism.

A fictional exploration of King allows Johnson to examine his own life as it intersected with the Civil Rights and Black Power movements. Johnson makes this connection clear in his editorial on King the dreamer; he calls himself a "child of integration" who had not fully examined King's influence on his life. King's integrationism "was replaced in me by black cultural nationalism before I fully had a chance to subject the black American goal of integration to philosophical examination." Because of his close personal affiliation with the politics of that time, Johnson uses *Dreamer* to explore and extend King's powerful influence on him through fictional and imaginative projection *into* King as a fictional character. The central character of *Dreamer* is King's bodyguard, who, having grown up in Chicago's Altgeld Gardens, cannot at first accept King's ideas about forgiveness and nonviolence. Gradually, however, the bodyguard, who also acts as King's double, learns to play King's role. Like a writer creating a character, the bodyguard mimics King's every movement while gaining respect for King's ideals and philosophy. As is characteristic of Johnson's fiction, the drama of cultural identity and politics serves as an illustration and exploration of the act of creation, an allegory of intersubjective aesthetics and the process of artistic self-creation.[2]

Through *Dreamer,* Johnson reverses his own ideological chronology through the bodyguard's ideological journey. Black cultural nationalism does not overwhelm the ideal of integrationism; it is instead national-ism that is overwhelmed. Johnson, in effect, rewrites his own history in *Dreamer* as his own artistic double is assimilated and eventually nearly transfigured into another version of King, his artistic subject. As a product of the Civil Rights era, Johnson imaginatively alters his fictional past to correspond with his pro-integrationist thinking today.

Through fiction Johnson hopes to extend King's influence and life in a world in which King "is strangely absent." In another article on King's influence, "The King We Left Behind," Johnson explores the irony of King's ubiquitous presence as a kind of deified and abstracted founding father whose face appears on stamps and whose birthday is now celebrated as a national holiday but whose message has been glossed over and even ignored. Johnson writes that King "suffers the curse of canonization." King, "this nation's most pre-eminent moral philosopher, . . . has been left behind" and forgotten. Replacing King's messages of nonviolence

2. Ibid.

and brotherly love are a "smorgasbord of oppositional agendas," including identity politics, which began with the call for Black Power in the late sixties. Johnson mourns this cultural reapportionment and wants to revitalize interest in King's theme of brotherhood.[3]

The Integrative Imagination

There are many ways in which King is the perfect subject for Johnson. Ideologically, spiritually, and philosophically, they are very similar. King's de-emphasis on race, his belief in spirituality (Eastern and Western) and in egalitarian American democracy are all echoed in Johnson's work. When King writes about race and identity, the words sound like they could have been written by Johnson: "Our cultural patterns are an amalgam of black and white. Our destinies are tied together. There is no separate black path to power and fulfillment that does not intersect with white roots. Somewhere along the way the two must join together, black and white together, we shall overcome, and I still believe it."[4]

Throughout his writing, his interviews, and his criticism, Johnson echoes and amplifies these ideas, albeit in a different cultural and historical context. Fundamentally antiseparatist, Johnson states that society is interdependent: "I really love Merleau-Ponty's idea that in the intersubjective social world each of us has a secret the other needs to learn. You can see my social back as I cannot. I can see your social back, and we move together towards enlightenment and completion, because we all do have different perspectives. But they do compliment and qualify each other."[5]

Indeed, for Johnson, creating art is a moral project: it allows writers to tell secrets across human divides. One of Johnson's central aesthetic strategies involves the imaginative transportation of the self into the other. Throughout Johnson's philosophical and critical manifesto, *Being and Race*, he urges writers to transcend their own limited perspectives and embrace as many different perspectives as possible to avoid racial and regional parochialism and to encourage interracial understanding and, perhaps, cross-cultural empathy. This is a fundamentally romantic impulse that stresses the mysteriously transcendent power of art. In *Defense of Poetry*, Shelley wrote,

A man, in order to be greatly good, must imagine intensely and comprehensively; he must put himself in the place of another and of many others; the pains and pleasures of his species must become his own. The

---

3. Charles Johnson, "The King We Left Behind," 8, 9.
4. Martin Luther King Jr., *The Words of Martin Luther King, Jr.*, 23.
5. Jonathan Little, "Interviews with Charles Johnson," 44.

great instrument of moral good is the imagination. . . . Poetry enlarges the circumference of the imagination by replenishing it with thoughts of every new delight, which have the power of attracting and assimilating to their own nature all other thoughts.

For the romantics, reason and imagination work together, "as the body to the spirit, as the shadow to the substance."[6]

For both Johnson and the romantics, the imagination's liberating powers have clear religious overtones. In 1974 Johnson wrote to his writing teacher and mentor, John Gardner, "flashy German philosophies like existentialism, and anti-philosophies like logical positivism, can't replace the experience of unity, certainty in ethics and faith in human values and purpose that was lost when the religious impulse began to die during the Industrial Revolution. . . . By religion I suppose I mean its root significance as *religiare:* to bind or unite. Now maybe fiction and philosophy (i.e. the head and the heart) can do this after all, or should." As this quote makes clear, Johnson uses the spiritual dimension of art as a romantic critique of the egoism, individualism, and rationalism of Western culture. Critics have surprisingly downplayed the spiritual in discussing Johnson's fiction, tending to stress instead Western philosophy and Johnson's debt to phenomenology.[7]

As a few critics have pointed out, Johnson's fiction and aesthetic have evolved into a pathway to the divine. Johnson is interested in showing his readers the sacred already existent within the network of human interrelatedness and connectedness. His art and criticism now imply the preeminence of the intangible spiritual realm as a foundation for ethical, political, and social strategies in ways that are more liberal humanist than postmodern. Johnson's motives resemble Tolstoy's, who writes, "The task for art to accomplish is to make that feeling of brotherhood and love of one's neighbor, now attained only by the best members of society, the customary feeling and the instinct of all men. By evoking under imaginary conditions the feeling of brotherhood and love, religious art will train men to experience those same feelings under similar circumstances in actual life." Further, for Tolstoy, "universal art" destroys separation between people and educates them "to union," showing them "the joy of universal

6. Percy Bysshe Shelley, *A Defense of Poetry,* 14, 1.

7. Charles Johnson, "Letters to John Gardner, 1974–1976," October 29, 1974. The exception to this is one of the most profound critical treatments of Johnson's work to date, William Gleason's "The Liberation of Perception: Charles Johnson's *Oxherding Tale,*" which does an excellent job accounting for Johnson's debt to Zen Buddhism.

union reaching beyond the bounds set by life." Unlike Tolstoy, whose perspective is predominately Christian, Johnson draws from a richly eclectic mixture of traditions that fuse primarily Eastern religious and spiritual beliefs with traditional Western aesthetic ideals, all the while viewing art as a nearly sacred vehicle for creating expanded awareness and beauty.[8]

Johnson, Romanticism, and Modernism

Ashraf Rushdy states that Johnson's second novel, *Oxherding Tale*, is "integrationist in a postmodern way [because] Johnson's concern is with developing a theory of subjectivity that dissolves what he says is the spurious concept not only of 'race' but also of 'personal identity.' " While partially right concerning his rejection of traditional Western notions of self and racial identity (as I will discuss throughout this work), defining Johnson as a postmodernist seems mistaken given Johnson's overarching views about art, culture, and politics. Instead of the postmodern "politics of difference" voiced by such leading African American intellectual figures as Cornel West, Johnson voices a more traditional aesthetic position that would like to see art as distanced from everyday political issues. In contrast, West writes that the new cultural politics of difference "embraces the distinct articulations of talented (and usually privileged) contributors to culture who desire to align themselves with demoralized, demobilized, depoliticized, and disorganized people in order to empower and enable social action, and, if possible, to enlist collective insurgency for the expansion of freedom, democracy, and individuality." These new cultural critics and artists place issues of power in the foreground to force change in the economic and cultural status quo.[9]

Johnson differs with this utilitarian view of art. For him, characters "are constructs, mental beings, who have more in common with mathematical principles than real people." Therefore, "when someone makes the claim that what we've [artists] done is empowered a certain class of people by giving them a representation of them on the page, I'm not sure what that means . . . I'm not sure that claim can be made as strongly as some people would make it." Throughout his writings and interviews, Johnson shows his discomfort with explicitly ideological fiction, which imposes restrictions on the artist's imagination. While West's and Johnson's positions correspond on many points—a desire to see more complex

8. Leo Tolstoy, *What Is Art?*, 190–91.
9. Ashraf H. A. Rushdy, "The Phenomenology of the Allmuseri: Charles Johnson and the Subject of the Narrative of Slavery," 386; Cornel West, *Keeping Faith*, 4.

artistic representations of African American experiences, a demystification of Eurocentric or Western ideals, and a more fluid construction of identity and nationality—they differ over art's social function. However, Johnson's attraction to integrationism makes his evolving aesthetic position fairly complex. This study will examine the tensions in Johnson's aesthetic as he wavers between an avoidance of and an attraction to the ideological.[10]

There are even times when Johnson's views align him with the most traditional of Western aestheticians. When Matthew Arnold writes of the power of the culturally elite artists in *Culture and Anarchy,* he states,

> This is the *social idea;* and the men of culture are the true apostles of equality. The great men of culture are those who have had a passion for diffusing, for making prevail, for carrying from one end of society to the other, the best knowledge, the best ideas of their time; who have laboured to divest knowledge of all that was harsh, uncouth, difficult, abstract, professional, exclusive; to humanise it, to make it efficient outside the clique of the cultivated and learned, yet still remaining the best knowledge and thought of the time, and a true source, therefore of sweetness and light.

Johnson echoes Arnold's words when he discusses his view that art is elevated from the ordinary: "I do think that art is elitist. It is an elitist activity. That may sound like a strange thing to say, but I will say it. When I sit down to write a book I put in the best thought, the best feeling, the best technique and skill I can muster . . . I believe that a great work of art is a special appearance in our lives."[11]

Yet, Johnson's position is curious in that through this elitist aesthetic medium, he promotes a nonexclusive, democratic, and spiritual unity more akin in spirit to the romantics than to the Victorians. Less like Arnold, and more like Coleridge and Shelley, Johnson emphasizes the imagination's power to unify and enlighten those of different classes or nationalities. The poet, according to Coleridge, "diffuses a tone and spirit of unity, that blends and (as it were) *fuses,* each into each, by that synthetic and magical power, to which we have exclusively appropriated the name of imagination." Further, the imagination "reveals itself in the balance or reconciliation of opposite or discordant qualities." The Beautiful is "that in which the *many,* still seen as many, become one." For Shelley, imagination "respects the similitudes of things." There is a tension, therefore, in Johnson's work between his self-professed modernist elitism concerning art

10. Little, "Interviews," 23.

11. Matthew Arnold, *The Portable Matthew Arnold,* 499; Jonathan Little, "An Interview with Charles Johnson," 180–81.

and his central message that existence is essentially egalitarian. Johnson's predominantly romantic aesthetic, which emphasizes the imposition of meaning, order, and unity upon experience through the imagination, further separates him from a postmodern sensibility that emphasizes separate linguistic and interpretive communities, discontinuities, randomness, and localization.[12]

Not surprisingly, given Johnson's retrospective tendencies, Johnson's closest African American literary and intellectual equivalent is the modernist Ralph Ellison. Ellison holds a similar integrationist position, though one less based in religion. In his 1981 introduction to *Invisible Man,* Ellison speculates on the role of the novelist in relationship to democracy, "For by a trick of fate (and our racial problems notwithstanding) the human imagination is integrative—and the same is true of the centrifugal force that inspirits the democratic process." For Ellison, novels can be rafts of hope, to serve society's democratic ideals and to help keep society afloat. In writing *Invisible Man,* Ellison sought to reveal human universals through his African American character as a means of "communicating across our barriers of race and religion, class, color and region," barriers that "prevent what would otherwise have been a more or less natural recognition of the reality of black and white fraternity." Johnson traces a similar integrative and fraternal design with his writing in attempting, first of all, to speak over the divisions that pervade contemporary society and its vexed discussions on race, education, and politics.[13]

Ellison dramatizes his integrationist beliefs in an unforgettable and metaphoric scene from *Invisible Man.* In this scene, the anonymous narrator mistakenly mixes ten drops of black coloring into the Optic White cans while working as an apprentice in the Liberty Paint factory. The result is paint with a telling gray tinge. Symbolically, neither race is pure after the intermixture. White becomes black and black becomes white. Because of this, argue Ellison and Johnson, an American democratic identity is a rich and fluid merger of cultures, styles, and beliefs. Adherence to such an improvisational and polymorphous national identity is hardly one promoted or accepted by today's many neoconservative pundits, such as Allan Bloom or William Bennett, whose vision equates national identity with a relatively fixed and hierarchical Eurocentric Western culture. While Johnson's thinking overlaps with their positions in his attacks on the divisiveness of identity politics, he ultimately diverges from such a position

---

12. Samuel Taylor Coleridge, *Biographia Literaria,* 12, 232; Shelley, *Defense of Poetry,* 1.

13. Ralph Ellison, introduction to *Invisible Man,* xx, xxii.

because of this central point. Where the neoconservatives see fixed principles of honor, morality, and a singular American identity defined in part by a standardized, Western-oriented educational curriculum, Johnson, building on Ellison's precedent, sees in America a dynamic, jazzy interplay of cultures and ideas, ever in-process and evolving and open to eclectic global influences.

Like Ellison, Johnson does not let his fundamental belief in integration blind him to the devastating effects of white racism on African Americans. Johnson is no mere American patriot, romanticizer, or utopianist. He does not espouse the cherished eighties, Reaganist belief in a color-blind society that refuses to acknowledge the impact of race and the legacy of racial prejudice in the United States. Throughout his fiction Johnson strikes a precarious balance between celebration, life-affirmation, and despair. While his fiction (especially his novels) usually depicts a final spiritual, psychological, and physical triumph for its African American characters, it also documents the pain and suffering necessary to achieve that goal. As the narrator of Johnson's short story "Consolation," a minister, relates, "it was easy to gather up the broken pieces of the people he served in a pretty grim picture—easy, in fact, to see all black being as, at bottom, a ghastly joke." The story documents the "sense that black history was, had always been, and might always be a slaughterhouse—a form of being characterized by stasis, denial, humiliation, dehumanization, and 'relative being.' "[14]

Although the temptation to dwell on victimization is understandable for the African American artist, Johnson wants to go beyond racial victimization in his art. Thus, Johnson reveals his tendencies as a moralist interested in improving society through art. "Responsible fiction discloses these triumphs as well as the failures; it offers, not the certainty that racial (and human) oppression will be resolved some day soon, as Gardner states in *On Moral Fiction* (there is, from my perspective, no such certainty), but the faith that we, and our children, can survive the minefield; can, in a word, make all minefields extinct." Hence, at the end of "Consolation," the minister is consoled and "cleansed" by a "vast, dreamlike hum: a uni-verse" of voices singing at a suicide's funeral. Johnson similarly sings, interweaving the tragic history of racial oppression and the possibilities for liberation, survival, and salvation into his polyphonic literary song.[15]

14. Charles Johnson, "Consolation," 97; Charles Johnson, "A Phenomenology of *On Moral Fiction,*" 153.

15. Johnson, "Phenomenology of *On Moral Fiction,* 155; "Consolation," 105.

Double-Consciousness

It is perhaps because of the rigidity of racial identity as it has been manufactured in America that Johnson so heavily emphasizes self-transcendence and intersubjectivity. In "A Phenomenology of the Black Body," Johnson envisions three unsatisfactory historical alternatives for constructing African American racial identity that are limited by their static and reactive nature. Johnson wants to diversify African American thinking on race, which he sees as primarily dominated by Du Bois's motif of "double-consciousness," a metaphor for the mind that splits American and "Negro" identity within one tortured African American body. In a review of a collection of essays about race and identity, Johnson challenges the assumption that African Americans are so tragically divided. He asks if this "is in fact an accurate account either of the experience of black life in this country or of racial consciousness anywhere." Instead of a dual consciousness, Johnson implies that the terms "poly-consciousness" or "cultural mulatto" have more resonance for contemporary constructions of ethnic identity. In the same review, Johnson discusses Stanley Crouch, author of one of the essays, "Who Are We? Where Did We Come From? Where Are We Going?" Johnson admires Crouch for recognizing the essential Americanness of black Americans and for espousing the heterogeneity of black identity.[16]

In line with this polyconsciousness, Johnson posits a revised conception of racial identity, one not tied to the constructions of race based on the troublesome Cartesian and Western dualistic mind-body split, which too often allies blacks with the body and whites with the mind. Johnson wishes not only to scrutinize popular discussions of race and racial identity, but also, he admits provocatively, to suggest that "it wouldn't be unthinkable to scrap the notion of 'race' in a country as genetically mongrelized as America. As a category or concept, race dissolves when ancestry is traced back fifty generations." In a statement that shows how inclusionist Johnson's vision of history is, he likens black American identity to a complex tissue "interwoven with all the diverse, global contributions that make the Republic a web of European, African, Eastern, and classical influences." Such a statement (which has obvious implications for shaping the canon) is dramatized six years later through fiction in his rendition of black American culture in *Middle Passage,* a novel whose subject is very much the American Republic.[17]

16. Charles Johnson, "The Color Black," 16.
17. Charles Johnson, "Whole Sight: Notes on New Black Fiction," 3–4.

Johnson undermines any argument that relies on essentialism, racial purity, or separatism. Replacing static constructions of identity, Johnson frequently posits a more fluid metaphor that begins presuppositionless and remains creative and improvisational. For Johnson, human identity is ever in-process, never complete—becoming a filmic "seriality of images" (*MP*, 169). This anti-Western perspective shows Johnson's debt to Buddhism, which argues that individual identity is amorphous, characterized by a constantly changing interaction of mental and physical processes. This thinking redefines the "self." In summarizing the Buddha's teachings on individual identity, Peter Harvey writes that "within such a conventional, empirical self, he taught that no permanent, substantial, independent, metaphysical self could be found."[18] Not surprisingly then, the concept of a deterministic racial essence is doubly problematic for Johnson, since an essence of any kind tends to limit possibilities, both for artistic and self-creation. Johnson's fiction is, throughout, a complex and sometimes self-contradictory homage to the possibilities and rewards of change and self-created freedom.

In bringing Eastern thought to bear on issues of American identity, Johnson is a rare combination of existentialist, moralist, phenomenologist, and Buddhist—his complex philosophical and religious orientation dovetails neatly into a spiritualized poetics of inclusive integrative diversity. As he states, "The point, which has been made elsewhere and more eloquently, is that our experience as Black men and women completely outstrips our perception—Black life is ambiguous, and a kaleidoscope of meanings rich, multi-sided." This sentiment is echoed in *Oxherding Tale*, when the narrator reports on the last thing he remembers before drifting off to sleep, "the last thing I remember of the Black World was Reb tending the fire, twirling a sliver of kindling; sank: a circle of flame; sank: a brilliant firewheel of inexpressible beauty" (*OT*, 97). So ambiguous, complex, kaleidoscopic, and ephemeral, black life's beauty is tantalizingly "inexpressible," uncontained by any singular essence.[19]

The Universal

Instead of rejecting the significance and importance of racial experience, however, Johnson feels that it is through the different experiences that the writer can access the universal, hence, in *Oxherding Tale*, the phrase "first person (if you wish) universal" (*OT*, 153). Given that controversy

18. Peter Harvey, *An Introduction to Buddhism*, 52.
19. Charles Johnson, "Philosophy and Black Fiction," 58.

has long surrounded use of the term *universal*—which began with white critics demanding that black literature always be universal—Johnson is provocative in reclaiming that term with his own modifications. Johnson argues that universals are "changing, historical, *evolving* and enriched by particularization." Through the window of black experience the writer can access universal themes that transcend time and place. In this wedding of the particular and the universal, Johnson echoes such romantic thinkers as Goethe and Schlegel, who emphasized in allegory and symbolism devices by which the artist can uncover the sacred and universal within the material. To dwell only on the material would, however, limit the range and scope of the work of art.[20]

Johnson applies what Edmund Husserl referred to as the phenomenological *epoche,* or the suspension of judgment to the process of artistic creation, to shatter one-dimensional racial stereotypes, perceptions that pervade our culture, especially those that calcify perception of the African American male. Husserl's slogan "To the things themselves" helped to found phenomenology's insistence that the perceiver experience as fully and as freshly as possible unconstrained by preconceptions or presuppositions. For instance, if portraying black characters, the artist must first abstain from and empty herself of all preconceived notions and assumptions about race; those notions must "be suspended, shelved, 'bracketed.'" "Aspects of the black world become, after the *epoche,* only the occasion for universal reflection." Once this is accomplished, the artist can then "note that Black subjectivity (memory, desire, anticipation) will stain them [consciousness and objects] with a particular sense." In the third and final phase, the artist can examine how the specifics lead to an illumination of a universal theme, perhaps a new universal, since all universals are simply shared meaning. This phenomenological process of artistic creation will result in what Johnson calls a "revitalized vision" in African American literature. Instead of the cartoonish caricatures of stereotypical African American characters featured on television sitcoms, literature will offer an alternative vision of dazzling diversity.[21]

This reverence for the particular, including the ethnic particular, clearly separates him from earlier African American proponents of what Houston Baker calls an "Integrationist Poetics," which held sway during the fifties and early sixties. Baker argues that Arthur P. Davis and others encouraged an assimilation into the mainstream of English and American

20. Ibid., 57. For an excellent discussion of romantic aesthetics, see Monroe C. Beardsley, *Aesthetics from Classical Greece to the Present,* 245–79.
21. Johnson, "Philosophy," 56–7.

literary forms, away from the distinct forms of "Negro" expression. Thus, "[Richard] Wright and Davis represent a generation whose philosophy, ideology, and attendant poetics support the vanishing of African-American expression qua African-American expression." Integrationist poetics is eventually replaced by Black Aestheticians who "seek to destroy [integrationist discourse] as a fatherly mystification of Anglo-male power." The paradigm shift offered by the Black Power movement displaces integrationist pluralistic ideals and a belief in the "oneness of all Americans and a harmonious merger of disparate forms of American creative expression" with a concern with developing distinctively black expressive forms for political purposes, since "Baraka and other artists who contributed to the establishment of the school [Harlem Black Arts Repertory Theater/School] felt that the perpetuation of African-American vernacular forms would aid the growth of African-American social and political autonomy in America." Black Aestheticians replaced integrationists' vision of a raceless and classless America with a "declaration of heterodoxy."[22]

Unlike the original integrationists, Johnson does not look forward to the disappearance of distinctive African American literary forms into the mainstream of white expression. Instead, Johnson works with such distinctively African American forms as the slave narrative and uses mythic African figures that recall an African spiritual heritage. Unlike the Black Aestheticians, however, Johnson does not remain locked in any one cultural or historical perspective; he draws from and blends African, Asian, American, and Western literary forms to promote his often implicit or nascent integrationist politics and poetics. Johnson's central aesthetic principle of "formalistic virtuosity"—a principle that I will address in chapter 2—exemplifies his simultaneous reliance on inherited cultural and literary forms and his avoidance of a sui generis stance. Committed to the "possibility that our art can be dangerous and wickedly diverse" (*BR*, 123), Johnson inverts the neat chronology of African American poetics that Baker constructs, reviving integrationist poetics with a difference. Through a well-thought-out and philosophically grounded aesthetic methodology, Johnson uses the particulars of racial experience to limn the universal and to emphasize the ties that bind.

Method

This study will analyze Johnson's work chronologically, to clarify the development of his career and aesthetic over the past twenty-five years.

22. Houston Baker Jr., *Blues, Ideology and Afro-American Literature*, 65–79.

In examining Johnson's art, my approach resembles George Levine's when he pleads for a new kind of formalism, "one that recognizes the ideological implications of the formal even as it values and deliberates over the nuances in the text." In imagining the aesthetic as, as Levine states, "a mode engaged richly and complexly with moral and political issues," I avoid artificially dividing the aesthetic and the ideological, a critical tendency that has led to an unfortunate emphasis among critics of African American literature. As Cheryl Wall points out, African American literature has often been read solely as ideology; it has been "misread as mimetic representation or sociology. In other words, the verbal text has been treated as if it merely mirrored the social text." Such a practice has been "inanely reductive." According to Madhu Dubey, literary critics have a history of dismissing "the works of black writers on the grounds that their ideological nature disqualifies them from the status of true literature."[23]

A writer vehemently opposed to these assumptions, Johnson has created a career in large part as an antithetical reply to these critical restrictions and categorizations. Johnson sees in art an invaluable and liberating way to plumb the depths of human experience on a number of levels at the same time: spiritually, emotionally, psychologically, physically, and historically. From the beginning of his career, Johnson has argued that serious philosophical fiction is too flexible, self-questioning, and polymorphic to have a consistent or predictable ideological perspective.

Without accepting Johnson's claims of ideology-free literature, I also seek to avoid the critical reductions he often defines himself against. In other words, I attempt to chart the ongoing interplay between the ideological and the aesthetic in his work without omitting his work's artistic achievement and development or its underlying and evolving ideological motivations.

Chapter 1 details Johnson's ambivalence toward the influences of the Black Power movement and the Black Aesthetic by examining his political cartoons. In Johnson's cartoons of the late sixties and early seventies, we can see him developing the independent satiric techniques he employs as a writer. Chapter 2 argues that *Faith and the Good Thing* (1974), Johnson's first published novel, was written to counter what he perceived to be the limitations of the Black Aesthetic and the protest tradition. Johnson's first novel unfolds his primarily romantic vision, stressing the unity of man with nature and the liberating and magical power of art. Chapter 3

23. George Levine, "Introduction: Reclaiming the Aesthetic," 3; Cheryl Wall, "Introduction: Taking Positions and Changing Words," 9; Madhu Dubey, *Black Women Novelists and the Nationalist Aesthetic*, 8.

discusses *Oxherding Tale*'s eclectic internationalism and expansive forays into Hinduism and Buddhism as epistemological departures to revise prescriptive ways of thinking about identity and race. Chapter 4 analyzes *The Sorcerer's Apprentice* (1988), Johnson's only short story collection, as a provocative counterpoint to his novels. Through his short stories, each of which will be paired with one of his novels, Johnson explores the horrific and unresolvable tragic aspects of African American history minus, in large part, the life-affirming possibilities of spiritual transcendence or mystical unity included in his novels. Through the exchange Johnson establishes between his novels and short stories, one can see the depth of his literary achievement and his desire to be ideologically open and formally innovative. Chapter 5 treats *Middle Passage* as the culmination of Johnson's aesthetic—the perfectly realized blend of formalist and ideological integrationism, and natural precursor to his novel *Dreamer.*

Throughout the chapters I examine issues of influence. Each novel is paired with a major literary precursor. *Faith and the Good Thing* is paired with Richard Wright's *Native Son; Oxherding Tale* with a twelfth-century Chinese parable, "Ten Oxherding Pictures"; and *Middle Passage* with Hermann Hesse's *Siddhartha* and Ralph Ellison's *Invisible Man.* Johnson self-consciously incorporates and modifies the central precursory text to help define his own position. In his first novel, *Faith and the Good Thing,* Johnson repeats and revises *Native Son* in a way that resembles and yet departs from Henry Louis Gates's complex theory of intertextual revisionism, which he calls "Signifyin(g)."

Gates uses the term *Signifyin(g)* to refer to what black writers always do when they "to create new narrative spaces for representation of the recurring referent of Afro-American literature, the so-called black experience." Their work is defined by a type of formal revision that Gates refers to as a form of critical parody, which includes repetition and revision based on the black vernacular tradition and the specific language use inherited from African religious figures. Black English vernacular is the "black person's ultimate sign of difference, a blackness of the tongue. It is in the vernacular that, since slavery, the black person has encoded private yet communal cultural rituals." In unveiling this self-reflexive black tradition, which includes specific black rhetorical tropes, Gates demonstrates how African Americans have developed a parallel discursive universe that is indebted to Du Bois's double-consciousness metaphor. Throughout *The Signifying Monkey,* Gates refers to Du Bois's quote about double-consciousness as a central organizing feature of his theory. He states, "The black tradition is double-voiced. The trope of the Talking Book, of double-voiced texts that talk to others texts, is the unifying metaphor within this book. Signifyin(g) is the figure of the double-voiced, epitomized by Esu's depictions in sculpture as possessing two mouths." As is characteristic of his integrative aesthetic, Johnson's pervasive metaphor of polyconsciousness blurs the metaphoric dualisms and sense of "signal difference" on which Gates's theory rests.[24]

Perhaps Johnson's often-repeated denials of distinct racial difference help to explain Gates's gatekeeping exclusion of Johnson in lists of significant contemporary African American writers. For instance, Gates's omission of Johnson's name from this list of contemporary African American writers is glaring. "He [Reed] has proceeded almost as if the sheer process of analysis can clear a narrative space for the next generation of writers as decidedly as Ellison's narrative response to Wright and naturalism cleared a space for Leon Forrest, Ernest Gaines, Toni Morrison, Alice Walker, James Alan McPherson, John Wideman, and especially for Reed himself."[25]

While much of Johnson's writing revises and therefore participates in the discourse concerning the representation of black experience, Johnson's use of literary and cultural influences is purposefully diversified beyond the specific language use that helps to define Gates's claims of black exclusivity. A close analysis of Johnson's relationship with mentor John Gardner as he wrote *Faith and the Good Thing* will reveal the interdependent weave of overlapping influences (black and white) as Johnson sought to break his ties to the conventions of African American protest fiction and expand the horizons of African American literature. Instead of repeating and reversing *Native Son* in writing *Faith and the Good Thing*, Johnson assimilates *Native Son* and Wright's integrationist poetics within his novel. Further, while Johnson does rely on black vernacular traditions in his first novel, he does so ultimately to undermine singular or bifurcated racial identification.

In a departure from Gates's theory of Signifyin(g), Johnson's use of previous texts and cultural influences more resembles the metaphor of integrative cross-cultural inclusion than metaphors dedicated to difference or doubling. This label of integrative inclusion is similar to, in some ways, Michael Awkward's intertextual metaphor of "inspiriting influences," or influence without the exclusive emphasis on African American literary precedent. Awkward revises Signifyin(g) to emphasize the harmonious system of literary influence between African American women's novelists. "It is this sense of bonding, of energetic explorations for and embrasure

24. Henry Louis Gates Jr., *Figures in Black*, 248; Henry Louis Gates Jr., *The Signifying Monkey*, ix, xxv.

25. Gates, *The Signifying Monkey*, 218.

of black female precursory figures, which distinguishes the Afro-American women's novels that are explored in the following chapters from competitive black male intertextual relations." Conversely, Johnson's intertextual process self-consciously embraces and integrates precursory figures across boundaries of ethnicity, geography, and historical periods.[26]

This study begins with a look at Johnson's work as a cartoonist, work that launched the career of an artistic polymath. He is an accomplished cartoonist, screenwriter, critic, and, of course, novelist. One can see even in Johnson's early cartoons his astonishing comic genius, his intolerance for hypocrisy, and his attempts to liberate himself from any one way of viewing race relations in this country. In Johnson's work one can find fascinating rhythms of liberation and entrapment and of optimism and despair as he meditates on individual identity and race. Johnson's fiction has always been provocative and at times breathtaking in its lyricism and insight and in its ambitious defense of the spiritual imagination. He is a truly interdisciplinary and international writer. I hope this book is the first of many critical works acknowledging Johnson's importance and achievement. And remember, at age 49, he is not done yet.

26. Michael Awkward, *Inspiriting Influences,* 2–14.

1

From the Comic Book to the Comic

Charles Johnson's Variations on Creative Expression

Charles Johnson began his artistic life as a cartoonist. Between 1965 and 1972 Johnson published over a thousand cartoons in a variety of publications, including *Ebony*, the *Chicago Tribune, Jet, Black World*, and the *Carbondale Southern Illinoisan*, and published two book collections, *Black Humor* (1970) and *Half-Past Nation Time* (1972). As a senior in college he also wrote, produced, and hosted a how-to-draw series for PBS called *Charlie's Pad*, which aired for a year, beginning in 1971.

In the early seventies Johnson grew disenchanted with the limitations of cartooning and moved on to teaching and writing. Nonetheless, Johnson's early cartoons offer a fertile field for analysis and anticipate, sometimes word for word, material in his later fiction. More important, Johnson's drawings showcase the phenomenological and daring satiric aesthetic he developed during the Black Power movement of the late sixties and early seventies. These cartoons reveal the interest he maintained in narrative development even within a characteristically discontinuous medium.[1]

1. Now, however, there is an emerging genre of comic book art, alternately termed the "graphic novel," or "sequential narrative." Examples of this genre include Jack Jackson's *Los Telanos* (1982), Will Eisner's *To the Heart of the Storm* (1991), and Art Spiegelman's *Maus* (1986). For a discussion of this genre and its criticism, see Dardess. For an extended discussion of Spiegelman's *Maus,* see Michael Rothberg.

The Political Cartoon and Phenomenology

Johnson's career as a cartoonist began very early. As a child, he says, "it was into drawing that I regularly retreated." Drawing held for the young Johnson "something magical about bringing forth images that hitherto existed only in my head." This passion for drawing led him to plan seriously for a career as a professional artist: "By my early teens I was determined to be nothing *but* a commercial artist." After completing a two-year correspondence course with artist Lawrence Lariar, Johnson was publishing cartoons in his high school newspaper and getting paid to draw illustrations for a company that made equipment for magicians. At the time, he says, "writing wasn't the kick for me that drawing was."[2]

Johnson enrolled at Southern Illinois University in 1966. While there he "drew everything—illustrations, panel cartoons, and two comic strips" —for the student newspaper, and political cartoons for the town's paper, the *Southern Illinoisan*. In a 1973 article about cartooning techniques, Johnson states the political cartoon appealed to him because of its "ability to deliver a statement in a striking image" and its power as "a definite medium for satire." It is "a visual editorial; it is the cartoonist's opinion. But also this: news analysis." As an opinionated statement, the effective cartoon "analyzes *ideas,* their contradictions and covert meanings," yet with a sense of restraint. Despite this cartoonist's credo of moderation, much of his article details the visual techniques of caricature and comic exaggeration. His emphasis on visual hyperbole undercuts his advice regarding "discretion," just as the images in his cartoons often graphically contradict the messages of the captions.[3]

An example of this paradox occurs in Johnson's definition of the "snowballing" technique for generating comic ideas, meaning "extending a situation to its logical and incongruous conclusion." His use of the technique is clear in an early political cartoon on Nixon and the Vietnam War. In the cartoon, Johnson replaces the "dove of peace" with a "ghoulish vulture" of death to symbolize and critique Nixon and Kissinger's false 1973 promises to reduce military involvement in Vietnam and to reveal the gap between their words and actions. Nixon is shown hunched over his desk in the oval office. A large, menacing vulture is perched on the back of his chair, leaning over him, drooling. Holding a newspaper whose headline reads, "Vietnam Deaths From New Air Strikes," Nixon asks his secretary, "What happened to those doves Henry promised me?" With

2. Charles Johnson, "Charles Johnson," in *Contemporary Authors Autobiography Series,* 223–43.

3. Ibid., 230; Charles Johnson, "Creating the Political Cartoon," 9–10.

their elongated noses, sagging posture, elevated shoulders, and high-lighted coloring, Nixon and the vulture are closely paralleled. Nixon is equated with the vulture's aura of death and bloodthirstiness, yet the tag line turns Nixon into a victim of Kissinger's deceptions. Neither the caption nor Johnson's definition of snowballing can contain the powerful message carried by the drawing itself, but the editorial commentary of this early cartoon clearly shows Johnson honing his satiric abilities.[4]

The comic techniques Johnson explains in "Creating the Political Cartoon" and explores in his many cartoons anticipate aspects of the phenomenological aesthetic he outlines in *Being and Race*, published in 1988. Johnson studied with Don Ihde at SUNY–Stony Brook in the early seventies as part of his Ph.D. work in philosophy and aesthetics, and he draws from Ihde's *Existential Technics* (1983) for the specific strategies of imaginative variation. These strategies, according to Ihde, are artistic methods for yielding "new perspectives" and for creating a "topography of possibility which is at the heart of phenomenological investigation." They include "figure/ground reversals, juxtapositions of contexts, [and] the isolation of dominant and recessive characteristics." Like satire, these tactics are deliberately designed to call attention to "sedimented convention" and to create deconstructive "shock, disjuncture [and] unfamiliarity." This systematic "logic of discovery" is used in different contexts by philosophers to gain distance from and insight into experience. As Ihde states, "This is in no way to say the phenomenologist 'creates' his phenomena in the way the artist does, but through the quasi-artistic process he employs, he discovers the structures of essential topographies."[5]

Apparent in his cartoons, the strategies of comic exaggeration, reversals, juxtapositions, and substitution also fuel Johnson's work in fiction. In his introduction to *Oxherding Tale*, Johnson outlined the six-year ordeal of writing that novel. After five years he lost his interest in the novel. Having a black protagonist was too predictable, since he had created a character who was too much like other characters in slave narratives. It was not until he started to experiment with imaginative variations that he became inspired. "Against my will I began to wonder what if the protagonist was mulatto—half-black, half-white—and thereby lived right on the dividing line between the races?" He further replaces the white male slave owner with a lascivious woman. Johnson was motivated to

4. Johnson, "Political Cartoon," 10, 13.

5. The phenomenological strategies are related to Gates's theory of signification. In *Figures in Black,* Gates writes that "signification can also be employed to reverse or undermine pretense or even one's opinion about one's status," 240.

begin a final revision and to consider adding stylistic touches from the eighteenth-century novel.[6]

Johnson and Baraka

One of the pivotal moments in Johnson's career as a political cartoonist seems to have come in the spring of 1969, when, feeling uninspired as an artist, Johnson attended a reading by poet, dramatist, and activist Amiri Baraka (then LeRoi Jones), one of the advocates for the Black Arts movement and the Black Aesthetic. The Black Aesthetic developed as the artistic implementation of black cultural nationalism, which called for the separation of blacks into their own nation, whether in the United States or in Africa. Baraka played a pivotal role in the development of the Black Aesthetic in his political activism and his artwork. Because of this, Baraka is often recognized "as the founder of the Black Aesthetic of the 1960s." In *Home,* Baraka says that "in order for the Black man in the West to absolutely know himself, it is necessary for him to see himself as culturally separate from the White man"; such an artistic separation would precede a physical separation to a new black nation in Africa.[7]

Baraka combined separatism with revolutionary fervor to form an insurgent poetics. An indication of Baraka's early aesthetic may be found in the lines "The Revolutionary Theatre should force change; it should be change. . . . The Revolutionary Theatre must EXPOSE! . . . White men will cower before this theatre because it hates them." Further, revolutionary plays should "cause the blood to rush, so that pre-revolutionary temperaments will be bathed in this blood . . . and they will find themselves tensed and clenched, even ready to die, at what the soul has been taught." Sixties activist Ron Karegna helped to codify Baraka's and others' exclusionist thinking into a theory of Africanist aesthetics that stands in direct opposition to a Eurocentric white aesthetic. This Black Aesthetic demands that black art be "functional, collective, and committing"; it must "expose the enemy, praise the people and support the revolution" in direct opposition to the traditional Western aesthetic demands for universality and alleged political disinterestedness.[8]

Hearing Baraka invigorated Johnson. He often writes of this experience. As a bored college student at Southern Illinois University, Johnson was

6. Charles Johnson, "Introduction to *Oxherding Tale,*" xvi.
7. Phillip Brian Harper, "Nationalism and Social Division in Black Arts Poetry of the 1960s," 236–37; Amiri Baraka, *Home,* 246.
8. Baraka, *Home,* 210–13; Ron Karegna, "Black Cultural Nationalism," 33–4.

experiencing a loss of artistic inspiration until that memorable night, when, he says, "this charismatic, brilliant black man was talking to *me*. I dragged home in the rain, dazed, seeing nothing on either side of me because my brain reeled with a hundred images for moving American comic art toward expressing the culture of people of color." Inspired by this experience, Johnson created his first collection of cartoons, *Black Humor,* in less than a week and is "profoundly grateful" to Baraka for his influence.[9]

He realized that what Baraka said about the need for an African American–based art was true. While Johnson recognized that there were a few African American cartoonists, no one was producing "books about black cultural nationalism, slavery, or African-American history." This led to a new, more politically activated aesthetic vision for Johnson. Indeed, Johnson recalls that his cartoons for the student newspaper "had grown so archly political in their call for revolution that my editor canceled a series of panels and told me to 'concentrate on everyday things.' " Caught up in the context of antiwar protest, he recalls breaking curfew and receiving "a lungful of tear gas thrown by the Carbondale police."[10]

Black Humor

The week after Baraka's speech was one of inspired creativity for Johnson. He produced *Black Humor,* a collection of eighty-nine cartoons that deals with a wide range of topics, all connected in some way to race and racial politics. This collection is Johnson's most intriguing production as a cartoonist in that it extensively examines North American racial politics during the sixties. Anticipating Johnson's interest in narrative development, *Black Humor* includes a cast of featured characters that reappear throughout the collection, such as an interracial couple and a black radical. Johnson introduces the major themes and characters in the first few cartoons, as is traditionally done in the first chapter of a novel.

Certain consistent images and running jokes hold the collection together as a unified "text." Through the comic techniques of imaginative variation, Johnson exfoliates several consistent themes: the perceptual gulf between the races, the dehumanizing effects of white racism, and the pervasiveness of racial stereotyping and racist mythology. Recurring, stereotyped images deeply embedded in this nation's past—white-hooded Klansmen, watermelons, and references to Uncle Toms—help Johnson quickly communicate his messages. Through his humor Johnson seeks to

9. Charles Johnson, "Where Fiction and Philosophy Meet," 48.
10. "Charles Johnson," 236–7.

liberate both himself and his audience from the pain of racism by calling up images of slavery and African American history and subjecting them to authorial control via his satiric aesthetic. Through his art Johnson seeks revenge on the injustices of the past.

The very first frame of *Black Humor* introduces the interracial couple who will appear throughout the collection in ten cartoons. In this frame (fig. 1) the couple is shown in a hospital, with the woman holding their newborn child. Under the African American father is the tag line "Rufus Junior!" Under the white mother, "Johnny!" From the start, then, the theme of the tragicomic gulf is introduced through this couple—they cannot agree on what to name their offspring since they are so different and so at odds over both heritage and language. In future cartoons, similar misunderstandings and unhappiness caused by their incongruous union will plague them. The white wife, for example, makes her husband birthday watermelon instead of a birthday cake and tells him one night in bed, "But I never expected you to be sexually superior, dear." This reflects the African American male's internalizing of the stereotype of black male sexual prowess (fig. 2). The couple, representing their races, have internalized devastating stereotypes. They are separated by a gulf made wider by the fact that they often can only relate to each other through reliance on racist mythology. That the two play such a significant role in the collection is telling: their priority shows Johnson's interest in exploring the intersection of the races, an interest he will develop more fully in *Oxherding Tale,* which treats an interracial couple in the antebellum South.[11]

In the second frame of the collection (fig. 3), we are introduced to another significant featured character—the black revolutionary who is distinguished by his *kufi* skull cap. Johnson references the Nation of Islam in this introductory cartoon and uses the *kufi* as a sign of the revolutionary leader, meant to stand for any number of Black Power approaches. In particular, the Nation of Islam, while under the leadership of Elijah Muhammad (1934–1975), advocated a separatist, anti-white doctrine. Muhammad argued that whites were "the offspring of the inventive devil Yakub, who was [at] one point a rising star in the world's first nation." Muhammad prophesied that Allah would defeat the white world in a war between Islam and Christianity and thus establish a theocratic utopian state on earth. Johnson makes a direct reference to Muhammad's racist beliefs later in the collection, when he shows an African American doctor preparing to operate on a white. The doctor says, "Muhammed [*sic*]

11. See Little, "Charles Johnson's Revolutionary *Oxherding Tale*" for a more in-depth discussion of Johnson's use of interracial couples in that unconventional novel.

Fig. 1. *"Rufus Junior!" From* Black Humor.

Fig. 2. *"But I never expected you to be sexually superior, dear."*
From Black Humor.

was right. White devils must be eliminated." Johnson distorts the facts
for comic effect, however, since the Black Muslims under the leadership
of Muhammad preached pacifism and chastised the Black Panthers for
advocating violence.[12]

The second frame of the collection parallels the first since it deals
with birth, yet the second offers the perspective of a black revolutionary.
The radical looks through the glass into the nursery where his child

12. John T. McCartney, *Black Power Ideologies,* 168. McCartney provides a discussion of Muhammad's political and spiritual philosophy and a summary of the
differences between Black Panther and Black Muslim attitudes toward violence, 170–
71.

Fig. 3. *Fist raised (no caption). From* Black Humor.

(presumably) lies. The radical raises his fist in the characteristic symbol of Black Power, and the infant child responds by doing the same, its tiny fist held above its head. This unannotated frame derives its humor from the unexpectedness of an infant adopting a radical political position, or any political position. Included in the cartoon is a white male, looking on with puzzlement and surprise—an audience within the cartoon itself. This theme of white surprise is sprinkled throughout the collection, as whites are shown humorously left out of the humor and the messages conveyed in the cartoons.

In a later cartoon dealing with infants and birth, Johnson adopts the perspective of the Civil Rights movement as led by Dr. Martin Luther King Jr. (fig. 4): "Free at last!" reads the caption, as the mother looks on in surprise at an infant who has escaped from his crib. In both the Black Power cartoon and this King cartoon, Johnson draws from familiar political images and popular rhetoric and substitutes different perspectives on the same circumstance: an infant adopting a political position. The motifs and characters that Johnson introduces in these opening cartoons will dominate the collection, especially when matched with the next cartoon, which is about the Ku Klux Klan.

In this cartoon, the first of many featuring images of the Klan, Johnson depicts an African American boy going with his mother to see a child psychologist. In one hand the child holds a Klan doll. Although it relies on simple comic reversal, this cartoon creates a powerful image that dramatizes the psychological trauma African American children can experience when they internalize white racism. The situation is repeated later in the collection when an African American adult, perhaps the boy grown up, is shown lying on a psychiatrist's couch holding a "White Power" sign. Read in the context of a developing narrative, this cartoon suggests that while the child matures, the damage caused by virulent white racism (as symbolized by its most institutionalized form, the Klan) remains unalleviated at the collection's ending.

The haunting specter of the Klan saturates this collection. In one cartoon Johnson depicts a Klansman painting an African American manikin white in an effort to whitewash emerging expressions of diversity and empowering black representations in the marketplace. Another cartoon illustrates the universality of the Klan mentality: an African American space traveler is greeted by alien Klansmen, while in the background a cross burns.

Images of the Klan intersect with the developing plot lines of the featured characters. For instance, the narrative of the interracial couple contains the Klan. One cartoon shows the African American husband

Fig. 4. *"Free at last!" From* Black Humor.

returning home from work, briefcase in hand. He is met at the door by his wife, who says, "Brace yourself, mother is visiting again." Sitting in the living room is an older woman wearing the familiar Klan hood. Another places the Klan in the context of suburbia—with the interracial couple in their backyard. The wife asks the husband if he has met the people next door yet. He looks on in surprise as he sees a Klan outfit hanging from the clothesline in the yard next door.

In a perverse twist on the interracial plot, another cartoon features the black revolutionary returning home to his African American wife. He

Fig. 5. *"Sho 'nuff, boss!" From* Black Humor.

suspects that his wife has been sleeping with another man. Gun in hand, he opens the closet door to find a Klansman hiding in the closet. This cartoon reverses expectations, and its highly unlikely climax uses humor to dramatize the double-dose fear of racial and sexual betrayal that plagues intra- as well as interracial couples.

Johnson, however, does not always picture the Klan in the position of haunting power. In a two-part cartoon he asserts authorial control over the Klan's haunting image (fig. 5). This pivotal cartoon shows a white-hooded Klansman praying before going to sleep. Kneeling by the side of his bed, he says, "Give me the strength to eliminate the inferior people ruining my nation." God answers in stereotypically southern African American expression, "Sho 'nuff, boss!" The Klansman's eyes are open wide in surprise and shock. Johnson deconstructs and deflates the Klanish worldview of white superiority and claims of divine sanction.

Cultural Nationalism

Despite Johnson's success at "exposing the enemy" in exfoliating racism through humor, his relationship to the black power radicalism is complex, even at this early stage in his career. Johnson's treatment of radicalism and its leaders is deeply ambivalent, tending toward parody. The satire

Fig. 6. *"Yes, I believe in African culture." From* Black Humor.

of black leaders begins early in *Black Humor.* One cartoon equates black power rhetoric with self-interested sexism (fig. 6). Johnson depicts the black radical pinning an African American woman against the wall at a party. She responds, "Yes, I believe in African culture. No, I don't believe in fertility rites." The radical's aggressive stance and the woman's angry expression reveal the radical's self-interested manipulation of nationalist ideology for sexual conquest, thus undermining his political sincerity and validity. In exposing the leader's inherent sexism, Johnson repeats and affirms black women's outrage at the gender hierarchy within the Black Power movement, provocatively labeled by Michelle Wallace "a vehicle for Black Macho."[13]

Johnson's own feminist critique is layered into interracial themes in a complex mini-narrative that involves two separate frames. In the first frame the black nationalist leader is shown lecturing to a crowd against the evils of integration and equating integrationism with Uncle Tomism. The last frame shows the leader leaving the auditorium by the back door to meet his date, who is a white woman. In this example Johnson plays with narrative in two ways: through the technique of multilayered cartoons and by tying the radical to the larger "plot" of interracial romance that is woven throughout the collection. This pictorial sequence similarly undermines the black revolutionary's sincerity and political validity: his involvement with a white woman in an interracial relationship directly contradicts his separatist nationalistic rhetoric. He is the race-betraying "Tom" that he warned against in his speech (fig. 7). Not only does the interracial plot serve to expose the destructive effects of white hatred, it also serves, for Johnson, to expose the hypocrisy and comic foibles of black radicals, whose actions speak louder than their words.

Johnson further parodies this hypocrisy in a cartoon in which an African American wearing a Black Panther–style beret poses for a CBS TV camera while in the middle of a race riot (fig. 8). The cartoon exposes the staged and manipulated quality of the movement as it "plays" to the public by exploiting its status as a national media draw.

Despite this satire, Johnson shows his divided sympathies through cartoons that alternately parody and support black radicals. In one example of empathic treatment, Johnson draws the black revolutionary persecuted by whites. He sweats at the sight of a vicious dog lunging at him, as a Klansman, who holds the dog on a leash, comments admiringly to his white companion about the dog's nearly human qualities. Johnson shows the same figure buying matches from a frightened white store

13. Quoted in Madhu Dubey, *Black Women Novelists,* 16.

Fig. 7. *"How'd it go tonight, Tom?" From* Black Humor.

clerk while holding a sign that reads, "Burn, baby, burn," indicating the revolutionary's power. Another cartoon shows a black trapeze artist symbolically refusing to catch his white partner. The varied sympathies in Johnson's cartoons show an artist alternating his messages, at times parodying black revolutionaries, and, at other times, showing their power or persecution in relationship to whites.

Black Aesthetics

Johnson's obvious ambivalence about the Black Arts movement is evident in his words as well as his drawings: "It is," observes Johnson, "that very same cultural nationalism—a serious roadblock for genuine black fiction and philosophy—that makes me uncomfortable, precisely because I was once one of its converts. Indeed, my first publication [*Black Humor*] would never have come about if it had not been for the black arts movement." Consequently, Johnson develops a way to get around the "roadblock" of cultural nationalism by creating a supposedly ideology-free, process-oriented aesthetics, drawing from the work of phenomenologists such as Edmund Husserl, Merleau-Ponty, and Ihde. Although Johnson understands the communal, political, and social reasons for the evolution

Fig. 8. *CBS (no caption). From* Black Humor.

of pro-black advocacy from Alain Locke's "The New Negro" (1925) to Black Power militarism, Johnson likens the Black Aesthetic to "fascist art in Germany during the 1930s" and to Kitsch. Negritude "in one incarnation or another . . . is a retreat from ambiguity [and] the complexity of Being," and is a suspect way of "controlling images" (*BR*, 20). Johnson reaches the conclusion that "all presuppositions, all theories must be suspended before experience and meaning can be brought forth in black literary art" (*BR*, 29). In the aesthetic dicta of cultural nationalism "is the very tendency toward the provincialism, separatism and essentialist modes of thought that characterize the Anglophilia it opposes."[14]

In two cartoons dealing directly with art in *Black Humor*, Johnson anticipates his later aesthetic pronouncements about the limitations of the Black Aesthetic. One cartoon depicts an African American artist in a gallery, palette in hand, standing in front of his completely black painting (fig. 9). He says to a white man, who seems puzzled, "It's life as I see it." The humor comes from two sources: the exaggerated application and enactment of the Black Aesthetic, which encourages black artists to create art solely through the matrix of racial identification, and the surprise of the white viewer, who is baffled by what this kind of racially exclusive art could possibly mean.

A cartoon with a different perspective on black art seems to convey the opposite message. This cartoon seems to chastise its African American artist for betraying his race, very much along the lines of the corrective and evangelical purpose of the Black Aestheticians, who sought to convince older and more conservative black artists to convert to their ideological perspective. In this cartoon an older African American writer hunches over his typewriter, drawing inspiration from an angelic muse who hovers above him. The muse is dressed in a Klan outfit, prompting an African American woman, perhaps his wife, to accuse him of being an Uncle Tom. Unlike the cartoon of the painter, this one seems closer to the Black Aesthetic's perspective in condemning the race-betrayal of older African American writers/artists, as they draw their inspiration from the most virulent symbols and manifestations of white hatred and racism.

Viewed together, these two cartoon-variants on art demonstrate the complexity of Johnson's response to the obligations and tenets of the Black Aesthetic, even while he was a professed "convert" to the cause of cultural nationalism. Viewed with the benefit of hindsight, these cartoons show Johnson torn between the nationalist thrust of his time and his discomfort with ideological rigidity. The moments of pro-revolutionary

14. Johnson, "Where Fiction," 48.

Fig. 9. *"It's life as I see it." From* Black Humor.

sentiment are carefully balanced by his satiric barbs against the movement. In *Being and Race,* completed in 1982, Johnson fashions his own supposedly anti-ideological phenomenological aesthetic, which "brackets" or eliminates ideology. "Philosophy is a neutral methodology"; ideology "closes off the free investigation of phenomena"(*BR*, 26). While the claim that philosophy—or literature, for that matter—can be ideologically neutral is problematic, Johnson's early cartoons illustrate his commitment to indeterminacy, to having ultimate artistic freedom, even if it means contradicting himself or creating an ideologically unstable or unusable text, counter to the requirements of the Black Aesthetic.

Uses of the Past

In a brief six-frame section devoted to slavery in *Black Humor,* Johnson achieves his initial objective of producing cartoons about slavery and history. This section views slavery from a comic angle to demonstrate the historical background of the racial humor that dominates the collection. By including slavery as one of his topics, Johnson reveals his historical interests as a writer. As in his novels, Johnson's depictions of slavery combine the harrowing and the humorous. In the first of the slavery cartoons, for example, Johnson recalls the Middle Passage experience by showing Africans in the hold of a ship, naked and packed together. One of the Africans says, "Say, why don't we have a sing-along?" This juxtaposition of innocent suggestion and horrific conditions results in an incongruent, pathetically humorous impact.

Another two-frame sequence in this section foreshadows an anecdote in Johnson's first published novel, *Faith and the Good Thing* (1974). The first frame shows a "Kentucky-gentleman" slave owner seated at his dinner table, being waited on by his slave. They hold between them a turkey wishbone. The second frame shows the slave having won his wish: the slave owner finds himself transformed into a black man, and the slave becomes a young white man. This comic reversal, or substitution, is repeated in *Faith and the Good Thing.* There, the magical and powerful Swamp Woman, fundamentally a trickster figure, who inhabits the swamps of Hatten County, Georgia, and who "had chosen death over captivity and made herself one of the living dead to torment her people's captors forever from the dank swamps, cackling to herself, working hoodoo, and conversing with spirits" (*F*, 18), is part of the oral folklore history of that region. In one of her most famous acts of magical vengeance, she is reputed to have granted "Massa Ferguson's" eight hundred–dollar wish to be young again by switching identities with one of his slaves, Jug. "Jug sold the Massa the very next day for two new muskets and a mustang, freed all his slaves, and threw a party in the Massa's Big House every weekend for thirty years until he died" (*F*, 18).

Multilayered, multiplotted, and imagistically complex, *Black Humor* demonstrates both the tentativeness and the commitment Johnson initially displayed in exploring through cartooning the often ignored areas of black American culture and history. In *Black Humor*, Johnson uses his biting visual satire to uncover and interrogate whatever examples of inequity, cruelty, and hypocrisy he finds, as he, cackling to himself like the supernatural witchwoman, delights in the power of the populist cartoonist to create disjuncture and scathing political commentary.

Half-Past Nation Time

In *Half-Past Nation Time*, Johnson uses the familiar comic strategies of reversal, substitution, and juxtaposition. Johnson here focuses on the militant Black Panthers as featured characters. More discontinuous than *Black Humor* in terms of narrative—there are no reappearing couples, for instance—*Half-Past Nation Time* relies less on repeated characters than on familiar and somewhat stereotyped media images, such as the raised fist or guns and ammunition belts for internal continuity. In comparison to *Black Humor, Half-Past Nation Time* explores increasing militancy in the Black Power movement during the early seventies, when Malcolm X's call to change society "by any means necessary" and Fritz Fanon's advocacy of violence as a positive force (in *Wretched of the Earth*) seemed to prevail. However, consistent with Johnson's alternating aesthetic approach, *Half-Past Nation Time* also contains images of revolutionary support, some of which draw attention to black poverty and economic oppression; drawing such attention and alleviating black poverty were two of the explicit goals of Huey Newton's Black Panthers.[15]

Despite such moments of sympathy and ideological harmony with the Black Panthers, *Half-Past Nation Time* begins with a decidedly ironic swing of Johnson's ideological pendulum. The title page displays a Black Panther revolutionary, shotgun in hand, fist clenched, standing with his foot on the neck of a white police officer, as if posing for a photograph after a successful big game hunt. This title-page introduction to the collection

15. McCartney clarifies this shift by focusing on the Student Non-Violent Coordinating Committee (SNCC), which had moved to a revolutionary ideology "in which both Black Separatism and the idea of a revolutionary transformation of the United States by any means necessary played a prominent part," 113.

Fig. 10. *Cover of* Half-Past Nation Time.

takes on a different meaning when, deep into the collection on page 69, the same Black Panther reappears paying the police officer for his cooperation in staging the photograph (figs. 10 and 11). What on the cover might have seemed a celebration of militant sentiment is revealed deeper in the collection as an ironic and comic commentary on a movement that exploits the media. Johnson extends the "narrative" of the original frame by showing its background story. This sequence satirizes the self-promoting, staged quality of the nationalist movement, as do cartoons in *Black Humor*. The comic variation that Johnson uses in the supplemental background frames is unexpected and significant; it reverses not only the cartoon's situation, but also its meaning, privileging satire and comic reversal over its potentially incendiary revolutionary message of "Kill the pigs!" That Johnson chooses to include this dramatic reversal as part of the title page

Fig. 11. *Photographing police officer (no caption). From* Half-Past Nation Time.

highlights his comic and satiric distance from ideological polemic, at least in this instance.

The opening cartoon in *Half-Past Nation Time* continues in this parodic vein. In this cartoon, an African American maintenance worker chastises a black revolutionary for missing the urinal, saying, "I sure hope your aim is better when the revolution comes." A similar cartoon elaborates on the schism between African Americans along class lines during a time of supposed racial unity and worker solidarity. This cartoon depicts an African American woman cleaning the Black Panther headquarters. The humor derived from this unannotated frame arises from the apparent sexist and classist hypocrisy of a movement oppressing women while espousing revolution and liberation from such constraints. Both cartoons show a fundamental split along class and gender lines between black revolutionaries and workers, female and male.

Fig. 12. *Posture/*Soul on Ice *(no caption). From* Half-Past Nation Time.

In *Half-Past Nation Time,* Johnson repeatedly attacks the sexist bias of male black nationalist leaders. Johnson exposes the militants' trivialization of women in a cartoon that depicts a man putting Eldridge Cleaver's *Soul on Ice* on women's heads to improve their posture (fig. 12). The visual message is clear: while pictures of male Black Panther leaders, including Huey Newton, hang on the wall, women are viewed as accessories, capable of translating Cleaver's words into trivial fashion aids but not of taking effective political action. As in the cleaning-woman cartoon, Johnson points out the second-class status of women within the black national-ist movement, exposing men's abuse of power through his exaggerated humor. According to Madhu Dubey, black women in the movement were assigned subordinate functions; further, "The Black Aesthetic figuratively trapped the black woman in the past, and barred her from participating in any new emancipatory discourse of blackness or femininity." Through his ironic visual commentary, Johnson makes essentially the same point.[16]

In a particularly intriguing cartoon, Johnson reverses the movement's gender hierarchy by depicting an angry woman arming herself with a rifle and spear and sitting in a rattan chair Huey-Newton style (fig. 13). This cartoon self-consciously revises Newton's famous armed-to-the-teeth photograph, substituting the woman for Newton and transposing her empowerment into the domestic sphere. The two other figures in the cartoon, presumably the woman's husband and son, appear frightened by this sudden assertion of male-associated militant power. The husband asks, "You wanna talk about it, Leslie?" while the son cowers behind him. The figure of "the woman" finally breaks expectations, and the results are frightening to the male observers and comically surprising to the cartoon's audience. Through this cartoon Johnson revises both the *Soul on Ice* cartoon, in which the famous Newton photograph hangs on the wall, and the photograph itself. Johnson moves the woman center stage, away from her marginal position as fashion accessory and sexual object, disrupting the habit of associating only men with militancy sentiment, thus fusing the feminist and Black Power movements. Even if still confined to the domestic sphere, the woman unbalances the men around her through her startling move into the realm of male privilege.

Itself "halved" by ambivalence, *Half-Past Nation Time* also contains some dramatic examples of Johnson's support for the revolution, in ways both direct and indirect. One two-page cartoon is more sorrowful than humorous. It is intended to convey reverence and pay homage to a fallen leader, namely Malcolm X, who was called Malik, meaning "the prince."

16. Dubey, *Black Women Novelists,* 20.

Fig. 13. *"You wanna talk about it, Leslie?" From* Half-Past Nation Time.

Fig. 14. *"There'll never be another Minister of Defense like Malik." From* Half-Past Nation Time.

With the annotation "There'll never be another Minister of Defense like Malik" (fig. 14), two black radicals watch Malik sink into a quicksand pit; all that remains of him is the black power symbol of the clenched fist. While there may be some ambiguity in the visual image—the fact that the two observers do not attempt to save Malcolm, the possible ironies involved in the quicksand image, given that Malcolm presumably died at the hands of Black Muslims angered at Malcolm's split from the Nation of Islam—Johnson's intent is not comedy. The prevailing mood of this cartoon is elegiac and sympathetic to Malik, the most prominent hero of the Black Power movement.

Half-Past Nation Time also evinces its revolutionary support in another, less explicit way. The collection contains six cartoons dealing with black poverty from an ideological perspective similar to the Black Panther's Marxist attack on capitalism. As McCartney writes, "Consistent with the ideology of Marxism-Leninism from which he borrowed so much, Newton argues that the tactics of the mass movement should not be spontaneous but must be guided by a disciplined vanguard party." Part of this carefully planned campaign included propaganda to "make the

Fig. 15. *"I may be a racist landlord . . ."* From Half-Past Nation Time.

masses conscious of their oppression" using the media "and children's breakfast and lunch programs like those the Panthers established in Oakland, California." Johnson iterates this Marxist attack on the wealthy in one cartoon in particular that pictures two whites dining at an expensive restaurant. One of the men says, "I may be a racist landlord exploiting my tenants in the ghetto but by God, it sure isn't **unprofitable!**" (fig. 15). The cartoon underscores the despicable motivations of the rich in their exploitative oppression of their tenants, similarly uncovered in Richard Wright's fictional portrayal of wealthy white tenement owners in *Native Son*. Johnson's satiric point drives home a propagandistic message that while Black Power–inspired accusations of exploitation are getting through, they are having little or no impact on the economic power structure. The wealthy, while acknowledging the truth of the accusations, are reveling in their materialistic gains. Such a cartoon, perhaps more than any other that Johnson has done, is designed to incite feelings of anger and longings for revenge and could easily play into the hands of the Black Panthers' propagandistic goals.[17]

Johnson also explores the harsh conditions of urban poverty by viewing it from the perspective of inner-city children. The most poignant cartoon pictures a black child on a front stoop surrounded by garbage being hugged by an enormous rat. Some other children walk by in the background and say, "It was love at first bite." The harsh twist on "love at first sight" emphasizes the degrading and unsanitary conditions that inner-city blacks must endure. In another cartoon, children are on a playground seesaw with a drug pusher (fig. 16). One of the children says, "That's what I like—a pusher who relates to the community and its needs." Like the cartoons with children in *Black Humor*, these frames derive their humor from the transposition of adult language into the mouths of children, as they adapt politically astute expressions to their own conditions. In the drug pusher example, Johnson substitutes *pusher* for *politician* to once more underscore the failure of the American political system to help protect these children, whose political power is, ironically, embodied in the form of a profit-seeking criminal. Both these cartoons and others dealing with urban black poverty show Johnson employing his satiric aesthetic to support a propagandistic Black Power ideological perspective. *Half-Past Nation Time*'s moments of ideological affiliation with Black Power hit home with more force than any of the cartoons in *Black Humor*.

Instead of settling into a predictable ideological stance, however, Johnson continues his parodies of Black Power rhetoric by lambasting another

17. McCartney, *Black Power Ideologies*, 145.

Fig. 16. *"That's what I like . . ." From* Half-Past Nation Time.

of its themes—universal black revolution. The first perspective, or variation, includes a black revolutionary being boiled alive in what is presumably an African native's pot. The native welcomes the revolutionary "home," calling him a brother. This cartoon's humor is derived from the use of the word *brother* and undermines support for anticolonialist, globalized, non-white appeals for unity, made by different voices within the Black Power movement, including Baraka, the Black Panthers, and the Republic of New Africa (RNA). In their internationalist stage, writes McCartney, the Black Panthers saw their struggle "as a struggle . . . for the liberation of exploited nations worldwide, especially developing nations." Pan-Africanists generally asserted the need for a worldwide unity among blacks to fight white colonialist oppression and to establish a liberated society. Through this cartoon, Johnson undermines any claims of international black solidarity necessary for the establishment of the new utopian community.[18]

In another variation on a similar circumstance, Johnson parodies white racial arrogance. In an extended mini-narrative, Johnson places a white in the native's pot. Thinking himself saved—and even deified—because he possesses a lighter, the white man is transported back to the tribe's leader. When the white proudly shows the leader his lighter, the leader hands him a bomb waiting to be lit. This cartoon satirizes and deflates white colonialist expectations and demonstrates that African natives have been empowered with nationalist sentiment. Underscoring this message, behind—and then out from behind—the leader's chair is the sign, "English go home."

In these two examples, Johnson varies the perspectives to parody two different populations' views—the Pan-Africanist expectations of the black revolutionary and the self-flattering notions of technological, godlike superiority of the white colonizing British. This pairing demonstrates Johnson's alternating comic stance; the first boiling pot sequence undermines global Pan-Africanist unity, while the second sequence asserts a global racial solidarity aligned against whites.

As in *Black Humor,* however, Johnson's ability to vary racial perspectives to open new topographies of meaning remains strong in his second collection of cartoons. For instance, there is a particularly intriguing cartoon that shows a white perspective in the midst of racial revolution. Coming home from work, a white male says, "Thank God, Lucy, I made it through another week without making a racial commitment" (fig. 17). Staying neutral in the racial battleground of the early seventies requires

18. Ibid., 142, 172.

Fig. 17. *"Thank God, Lucy . . ." From* Half-Past Nation Time.

intense effort; legs spread apart, the man strives to maintain his balance. The comedy arises from the husband's exaggerated relief—he has not taken any position, yet the strain of maintaining neutrality is evident from his expression and posture—and from the cartoon's pictorial allusion to Thomas Jefferson, whose racial balancing acts have been much discussed by African American historians. Johnson visually accentuates the balance motif by including a mobile in the center of the cartoon. The mobile symbolically contains one black panel and five white panels, suggesting the minority status of African Americans. The traditional perception of the United States as belonging to white America is under siege during this tumultuous time in the country's history; the power balance that the mobile symbolizes is threatened during this revolutionary period. When viewed in the context of the rest of *Half-Past Nation Time,* with its surplus of guns, fists, riots, flying bullets, and police harassment, this cartoon shows middle-class white America struggling to maintain a social disequilibrium that may be no longer possible and is certainly not courageous.

In some ways this cartoon is emblematic of Johnson's own comic balancing act. His doubled-edged, ironic humor, both in *Black Humor* and *Half-Past Nation Time,* evidences his attempts to remain ideologically neutral and fundamentally uncommitted to any single perspective, while, at the same time, vacillating between racial and political perspectives. And this strain, as I will discuss below, may have compelled Johnson to abandon political cartooning and work his way back to explicit political satire after first perfecting his craft of writing innovative philosophical fiction.

Further Transformations

In 1970 Johnson's cartoons move away from issues of race and politics and become immersed, as he himself was, in issues of spiritual enlightenment. Johnson created *It's Lonely at the Top,* an unpublished collection of cartoons devoted entirely to Eastern philosophy and religion. A precursor text to *Oxherding Tale* especially, which uses twelfth-century Chinese Buddhist's Kaku-an Shi-en's *Ten Oxherding Pictures* as a source, *It's Lonely at the Top* features a white character named Herman, who, along with a companion, quests after wisdom and truth. By the time Johnson wrote *Oxherding Tale* (1982), he had reinserted an African American into the protagonist's role.

Despite the change in topics and emphasis, however, from the political humor of *Black Humor* and *Half-Past Nation Time,* Johnson retains a similar satiric approach in *It's Lonely at the Top.* Instead of preaching the virtues of Eastern meditation and recommending it as the singular path to enlightenment and truth, Johnson the humorist uses this subject as an opportunity for satiric reflection and familiar comic reversals. One irreverent cartoon, for example, depicts Herman and his companion on the mountaintop with a sign advertising their expertise. Other cartoons similarly parody the pretentiousness and self-righteousness of the holy seeker of truth. One depicts Herman in meditation being irreverently mimicked by a parrot who repeats his monotonous chants. Another shows Herman reveling in hearing a statement propounding his enlightened state echoed back to him across the ravines and mountains. These cartoons, and others in this collection of twenty-two, reveal in comic fashion Herman's ineffectiveness in the transcendental seeker's attempt to abolish egoism and to obtain a higher spiritual realm.

While much of the collection is devoted to parodying Herman, there are several cartoons that reveal a sympathy with his spiritual goals. One cartoon shows Herman hit in the head with a football while trying to meditate on the familiar mountaintop. In another, Herman and his companion try to avoid being disturbed by other seekers of wisdom by carving hostile messages into the mountainside where they are meditating.

As the collection demonstrates, Johnson's interests in philosophy and in Eastern religions were growing. He started to explore new genres. His career plans changed during his senior year in college. "I was going to be a philosophy teacher who wrote novels on the side, sort of like Bill Gass," but in 1973 he gave up cartooning because, he says, "working with images in such a limited way was frustrating. The expressions I wanted as I got older were impossible. . . . So I did philosophy throughout graduate school and developed a style of thinking that I couldn't explore expansively in the form of comic art. This led me to the novel." In a more recent interview, Johnson adds, "The reason I left behind being a cartoonist was because I was looking for the means that would allow me to express the most I could." Johnson continues, "I don't think you can substitute, just because it's a 'text,' an African-American comic book for Melville's *Benito Cereno*."[19]

In other interviews, Johnson talks about the superiority of writing over drawing and even over film for deep philosophical and artistic expression and exploration. "Somehow," Johnson states, "the literary work of art is closer to the life of the consciousness." Writing offered Johnson the cartoonist a more expansive artistic genre that would allow him to convey

19. Marian Blue, "An Interview with Charles Johnson," 2; Ken McCullough, "Reflections on Film, Philosophy, and Fiction: An Interview with Charles Johnson," 119; Little, "An Interview," 181.

greater complexity of value and meaning—the sense that "the meaning of things is open-ended, constantly changing, [and] evolving." This realization merges form and philosophy since there is no way to capture consciousness in a single representation. "[W]e are," writes Johnson, "after all, beings who must fashion moment by moment what meaning our lives will have, beings in *process* who are subject in a single lifetime to change, transformation, self-contradiction, and constant evolution." Yet the similarities in the satiric techniques between Johnson's cartooning and his writing belie the clear distinction Johnson often makes between the high art of literature and the low art of cartooning.[20]

Cartooning Revisited

After more than twenty years away from drawing, Johnson seems to be re-creating himself again by returning to political cartooning. Johnson draws monthly for the *Quarterly Black Review* and uses his cartoons to comment on racial politics, just as he did at the start of his artistic career. The features that characterized his early satiric aesthetic—including varying perspectives, substitution, reversal, and surprise—are still evident. Now, however, Johnson's cartoons seem somewhat more ideologically slanted than earlier in their espousals of integrationism and, concomitantly, less incisive in their attacks.

In recent issues of *Quarterly Black Review,* Johnson satirized both the recent Colin Powell phenomena before his announcement that he would not run for president and Nation of Islam leader Louis Farrakhan's speaking at the Million Man March. By choosing black leaders from opposite ends of the ideological spectrum to satirize, Johnson shows his commitment to maintaining a certain amount of ideological flexibility. The first cartoon depicts a black tourist family looking out over Mt. Rushmore, which now includes Colin Powell's likeness. The father says, "We read his book and saw the opinion polls, so we shouldn't be surprised. . . ." Instead of parodying Powell, however, the cartoon is a mild exaggeration of the Powell phenomena and incongruous extension of Powell's popularity: he is elevated to the level of the most revered American presidents even before he announces his candidacy. The cartoon, which is not particularly memorable, is diluted as political satire for two main reasons: it does not address Powell himself but instead evinces an underlying support for Powell. The woman wears a "Powell '96" button, which, while it helps

20. McCullough, "Reflections," 122–23; Charles Johnson, "A Phenomenology of the Black Body," 603.

to explain the cartoon's narrative, also tends to nullify the satiric thrust, since it puts the family in collusion with the phenomena.

This collusion may not be accidental. In statements about recent politics, Johnson's support for Powell is clear. For instance, in criticizing Toni Morrison's and Alice Walker's depictions of black men in their fiction, Johnson has remarked, "Some of the portraits of black men in those books are so limited and one-profiled, as opposed to thirty or forty images of black men, that they don't seem moral to me. It's not just Walker. You could also talk about Morrison. You do not see black men like Colin Powell or W. E. B. Du Bois or astronaut Ron McNair or Frederick Douglass. It's an extremely narrow range of human beings. You basically see black men who are fuck-ups."[21]

Politically, Powell would seem to embody for Johnson his moderate, integrationist ideals and stress on certain human values that the Republican party has appropriated for their campaign rhetoric. Yet, as usual, Johnson wants to distinguish between universal human and partisan values. In a recent article for *National Minority Politics,* a magazine whose editorial policy emphasizes "compassionate conservativism" (a stance similar to Powell's), Johnson advocates for "middle-class" values: "They are *human* values. Call them conservative, if you like, but once we dispense with labels they will be seen simply as the formula for successful living at any time." These values include the work ethic, discipline, education, family, and "the capacity for self-sacrifice and religious piety." These very values are depicted in Johnson's art in his recently published teleplay "The Green Belt," in which a young African American male rejects the temptations and dangers of gang life for the self-restraint, discipline, and artistry of the martial arts. In the "religious quiet" of the martial arts studio, the young male executes "a beautiful performance," in which he does "a fine interpretation of the form," and earns the admiration and respect of those closest to him.[22]

Given these values, a biting satiric attack on Farrakhan would seem logical, but even his Farrakhan cartoon demonstrates a muted satiric performance. While Farrakhan is making his speech to those gathered in Washington for the Million Man March, one of the members of the Nation of Islam whispers to him, "Psst, Boss . . . lighten up on the numerology, okay?" The mild satire pokes fun at Farrakhan's use of predictions and exhortations using numerology and hints at disagreement among Black

21. Little, "An Interview," 175.
22. Charles Johnson, "Absence of Black Middle-Class Images Has Global Impact," 22; Charles Johnson, "The Green Belt: A Play for Television," 578.

Muslims. However, given the incendiary topics associated with the controversial leader, including Farrakhan's extreme statements on ethnicity, Johnson's choice of satiric topics seems particularly evasive and noncommittal. The two recent cartoons, though different, both lack the satiric bite that characterized his earlier comic assaults on black leaders. Perhaps Johnson's earlier ambivalent conversion to black cultural nationalism created an aesthetic and ideological tension in Johnson that fueled his satiric efforts and allowed him to parody black leaders with such ruthlessness (and to sympathize with Black Power issues) as he struggled to define his own finally integrationist position.

Yet there is a contradiction. If Johnson had been utterly true to his own claims of multisided political neutrality in those early years as a political cartoonist, he would have produced attacks on King's integrationist position with as much satiric vehemence as he directed toward the stance of black nationalist leaders. The closest Johnson comes to parodying King's positions—which are fraught with their own difficulties—is in the "Free at last" cartoon, which is an extremely distanced treatment of King, and, in effect, no parody at all. Despite his ambivalence toward black cultural nationalist positions, Johnson's satiric avoidance of integrationist rhetoric may have been an early, if indirect, indicator of his ideological preferences.

Postscript

In returning to cartooning, Johnson may be trying to live up to his own aesthetic criteria, which stress artistic virtuosity, both within literature and across artistic media. In an interview Johnson stated,

> Every writer, in principle, should be able to write in as many forms as possible. Finally, all these forms of expression are unified in a personality, in the artist himself, because some things he can get to only through images, and some things he can get to only through imaginative uses of language, and some things he can get to only through conceptual approaches, or analysis. For me, then, each is a different order of expression and all are on a parity. It shouldn't, for the writer, be much trouble to switch—it's just a slightly different cognitive style for each, variations on creative expression.[23]

In an extension of Johnson's cartooning strategies, his first novel, *Faith and the Good Thing* (1974), includes a female protagonist who embodies Johnson's revered principle of artistic variation as she moves out of the constrictions placed on her by her environment and adopts

23. McCullough, "Reflections," 119.

different perspectives through the magic of her integrative imagination. Through this liberated character, Johnson inscribes the history of his own transformations as he experiments with new modes of expression and new perspectives that are still unified by his distinctive artistic personality.

2

Liberatory Aesthetics

Faith and the Good Thing,
the Conjurer, and
Native Son

J ohnson's switch from cartoonist to writer was sudden, but he soon proved to be a dedicated and prolific novelist. While earning his Master's degree in philosophy from Southern Illinois University (1970–1972), Johnson wrote six unpublished novels at the rate of one per semester. In *Being and Race,* Johnson labels the first of his three unsuccessful novels an imitation of the naturalistic style of James Baldwin, Richard Wright, and John A. Williams, while the next three were indebted to the Black Aesthetic. Johnson says, "I had no interest in revisiting their fictional worlds ever again" (*BR,* 6).

In hindsight, Johnson realizes that in naturalism are "profound prejudices about Being, what a person is, the nature of society [and] causation" that "made my characters dull and predictable in their inner lives and perceptions of the world." Johnson felt that the conventional point of view of naturalistic writing "put curious limits on narrative voice and language" and held his "imagination close to the ground" (*BR,* 6). In other words, neither adopting the naturalistic style nor adhering to the Black Aesthetic allowed Johnson the artistic freedom he needed to create what he considers truly philosophical and exploratory fiction. Beyond "the existential stories of Wright, the Freudian adventure of Ellison, and the beautifully transcendental fiction and poetry of Jean Toomer," Johnson

54

says "[I] found little I was willing to call genuine philosophical black literature."[1]

In *Faith and the Good Thing,* Johnson creates a character, Faith Cross, who is finally free to create meaning, value, and a coherent identity against a background of racial, economic, and sexist oppression. Faith accomplishes her aesthetic and spiritual liberation through a gradual conversion from victimized naturalist and realist character to empowered conjurer and trickster figure. Using this distinctive and immediately recognizable heroic figure has clear ideological implications. Madhu Dubey writes that

> black feminist critics are increasingly turning to metaphors derived from folk culture, such as conjuring, specifying, quilting and laying on of hands, in order to theorize the distinctive literary and cultural practices of black women. This recent theoretic privileging of folk cultural models may be traced to Black Aesthetic discourse, which constructed folk forms as the origin of a uniquely black cultural practice . . . folk (and especially oral) forms were valorized by Black Aesthetic critics as the most effective means of representing a unified and essentially black communal consciousness.

Even when using African American folk forms, however, Johnson reverses or modifies their ideological implications. It is through the mythic and conjuring Faith Cross that Johnson crosses or subverts the expectations of the Black Aesthetic critic; at the novel's end, Faith becomes an implicit argument more for artistic and philosophical freedom than for unified black communal consciousness. She becomes a goddess of phenomenology's "free variation," instead of primarily an African goddess. Indeed, Faith ends the novel curiously isolated and neutralized as a revolutionary force.[2]

Conjuration

Despite Johnson's final formalistic and ideological reversals, this folk-based vision aligns Johnson's first published novel with an emerging tradition of feminist African American literature of the period. In Marjorie Pryse's introduction to *Conjuring,* a study of African American women's writing, Pryse says, "In the 1970s and 1980s, black women novelists have become metaphorical conjure women, 'mediums' like Alice Walker who make it possible for their readers and for each other to recognize their common literary ancestors." This vision, which is "based on magic, oral

1. "Charles Johnson," 223–34.
2. Dubey, *Black Women Novelists,* 5.

inheritance, and the need to struggle against oppression," is identified as the intimate possession of "black women alone." These writers, beginning with Zora Neale Hurston in *Their Eyes Were Watching God* (1937), countered racist and sexist oppression through the " 'magic' of authority that makes storytelling." The narrator of *Their Eyes Were Watching God,* for example, has the ability to create a world, use magic, conjure up the past and the dead, and revivify the "ancient power" of black women ancestors.[3]

Many critics, in focusing on tensions between feminist goals and male-dominated black nationalist agendas, claim that critiquing of the gendered assumptions of Black Aesthetic critics and writers was performed solely by women. However, Johnson uses *Faith and the Good Thing* to accomplish many of the same ends. In his novel he counters urban alienation, racial oppression, nihilism, and marginalization with the power of conjuring and aesthetic creation in the African American oral folk tradition, thereby reestablishing the broken generational and spiritual links between generations. At the end of the novel, Faith Cross takes her place as the conjurer, trickster, religious leader, mythmaker, and the artist who subverts the conventional hierarchies of race, class, and power—and does so as a female character, although such distinctions of sexual identity are rendered less significant given her transformative, identity-switching powers.

Johnson's final move is creating Faith as a polymorphic figure consistent with the conjurer's powerful legacy in African American mythology. John Roberts makes the argument that the conjurer carried the Africanist religious worldview into the antebellum slaveholding context, where spiritual leaders were forbidden to practice. Enshrined as folk heroes, these conjurers were referred to by many different names, including "root doctor, herb doctor, herb man, underworld man, conjure man, and gofuhdus man." The conjurer was "the professional diviner, curer, agent finder, and general controller of the occult arts." Endowed with extraordinary spiritual knowledge and power, conjurers possessed "a superior life-force"; they were the enslaved Africans' religious specialists. Conjurers helped displaced Africans to maintain "full ontological being."[4]

These religious specialists had a tremendous symbolic and cultural significance on many levels. As W. E. B. Du Bois writes, the priest "early appeared on the plantation and found his function as the healer of the

3. Pryse, Marjorie, "Introduction: Zora Neale Hurston, Alice Walker, and the 'Ancient Power' of the Black Woman," 5–14.

4. John Roberts, *From Trickster to Badman,* 65–104; Norman E. Whitten Jr., "Contemporary Patterns of Malign Occultism among Negroes in North Carolina," 409; Roberts, *From Trickster,* 74–80.

sick, the interpreter of the Unknown, the comforter of the sorrowing, the supernatural avenger of wrong, and one who rudely but picturesquely expressed the longing, disappointment, and resentment of a stolen and oppressed people." Roberts summarizes this figure's symbolic significance: "As individuals whose knowledge and power emanated from a source outside the slave system, conjurers were sources of power and knowledge that could be neither controlled nor usurped by the masters. Therefore conjurers afforded enslaved Africans a focus for creating oral expressive traditions to transmit a conception of behaviors alternative to those fostered by existence under European domination." The heroic deeds of the conjurers were recalled and celebrated in "conjure tales," which were frequently repeated and "reflected a lack of black acculturation in European-American values." In these tales the conjurers were "portrayed as individuals who, in curing illness, combined their knowledge of the medicinal properties of plants, herbs, roots, barks, animal substances, and so forth with mysticism." Telling the conjurer tales was an act of rebellion against the cultural hegemony of the white masters and a means of communal preservation and empowerment.[5]

In examining the supernatural, mythic trickster figures in West African religions, Robert D. Pelton makes the trickster synonymous with the polymorphous conjurer figure. The trickster is "the mediator who spells out the cosmic designs in human language"; as spiritual leaders they "crystalize the hidden shape of the universe." The trickster is both of the human and of the supernatural world, able to move between the two, primarily to educate and liberate humankind. "In symbolizing," writes Pelton, "the transforming power of the imagination as it pokes at, plays with, delights in, and shatters what seems to be until it becomes what is, he discloses how the human mind and heart are themselves epiphanies of a calmly transcendent sacredness so boldly engaged within this world that it encompasses nobility and messiness." This sacred trickster and prankster thus uses humor and "play" to "shatter what seems to be" and to liberate its audience from conventions, similar to the way Johnson uses humor in his cartoons. Faith becomes an artist figure, playing at the borders of convention, reality, and society. Not only does Faith become the sacred, supernatural trickster and conjurer figure, she steps into the role of comic interpreter, free to transcend and subvert any boundaries that humans have constructed. At the end, she becomes the instructive sacred pathfinder—limited only by the play of her imagination, which, as it turns out, recognizes almost no limitations at all. Like the trickster Pelton

5. W. E. B. Du Bois, *The Souls of Black Folk*, 144; Roberts, *From Trickster*, 66–97.

describes, she is the one who can, "change forms as easily as he can tell lies. To pin him to one meaning is to annul his power to link the many levels of experience and to destroy the imaginative irony that he incarnates. His dance pulverizes the univocal and gives voice to teach of the 'surprises of the actual.'" In invoking such a central West African spiritual figure, Johnson draws from the deepest wells of sacrosanct African heritage and fulfills his religious impulse. That he emphasizes the trickster's ultimately "surprising," "playful," and polymorphous character reveals the extent to which Johnson has transcribed his own often comically surprising aesthetic vision onto his rendition of this central mythic figure.[6]

Johnson and Wright

Despite his disdain for Wright's stylistic influence, Johnson's first novel partially fulfills Wright's formalist and ideological integrationist ideals. In "Twelve Million Black Voices," Wright argues, "The differences between black folk and white folk are not blood or color, and the ties that bind us are deeper than those that separate us." The diminishment of racial oppression will strengthen the ideal of American unity across racial lines. In his discussion of African American literature in "The Literature of the Negro in the United States," Wright looks forward to the merger of black folklore, spirituals, and songs into what he calls American expression, since this will signify the end of the Negro's alienated (nonintegrated) state of estrangement and economic oppression. With strong utopian overtones, Wright anticipates this formalist amalgamation, since it will symbolize the oneness of humanity: "If . . . our expression broadens, assumes the common themes and burdens of literary expression which are the heritage of all men, then by that token you will know that a humane attitude prevails in America towards us."[7]

In "Blueprint for Negro Writing," Wright's integrationist ideals are reflected in his insistence on formalist diversity. He urges Negro writers to

6. Robert D. Pelton, *The Trickster in West Africa*, 23–45, 33–4, 224.

7. Richard Wright, "Twelve Million Black Voices," 240; Richard Wright, "The Literature of the Negro in the United States," 149–50. In a compelling and creative comparison, William R. Nash explored the similarities and differences between *Faith and the Good Thing* and Theodore Dreiser's *Sister Carrie* in "Two Views of Desire: Charles Johnson's *Faith and the Good Thing,* Dreiser's *Sister Carrie,* and the Idea of Antinaturalism." Nash concluded his comparison by arguing that despite the similarities between the two characters, Faith's freedom at the end of the novel shows Johnson's belief in free will, as opposed to Dreiser's belief in determinism. This freedom is won, largely, by Faith's rejection of desire.

avoid the "stunted plants of Negro nationalism" by approaching Negro life "from a thousand angles, with no limit to technical and stylistic freedom"—a statement that compellingly corresponds to Johnson's own Gardneresque aesthetic of formalist virtuosity and genre crossing. Like Johnson, Wright states that Negro writers must not let their artistic pursuits be overwhelmed by polemic. The Negro writer must also seek to increase his commitment to "the collective sense of Negro life in America," and overcome "the present mode of isolated writing and living. . . . It means that Negro writers must have in their consciousness the foreshortened picture of the *whole,* nourishing culture from which they were torn in Africa, and of the long, complex (and for the most part, unconscious) struggle to regain in some form and under alien conditions of life a *whole* culture again."[8]

In *Native Son,* Bigger longs for the aesthetic power that would connect him with this holistic nourishing culture and with the enriching conduits of racial wisdom. In *Faith and the Good Thing,* Faith fulfills this longing through the very folkloric forms that Wright wishes to see merged into American expression. Although certainly not writing according to Wright's overarching ideal of Marxist consciousness, Johnson fulfills Wright's ideas about the artist's power to create inspiring myths and symbols by first embedding aspects of *Native Son*'s naturalism and Chicago setting and Wright's integrationist aesthetics within *Faith and the Good Thing.*

Before Faith can attain her desired liberation as a magical force of African American folklore, and then as a liberated artist, she must move through the racial landscape exposed in *Native Son*—the naturalistic socioeconomic nightmare that constructs African American identity in purely reactive and mechanistic terms. These characters inhabit a painful wasteland dominated by, as Wright laments, "the moral horror of Negro life in the United States." The list of racial crimes against Faith and her family is extensive. Faith's father is killed by three whites in a racially motivated attack when she is a child. When her mother dies, Faith travels north to Chicago, where she is robbed, beaten, and forced to become a prostitute to support herself. She becomes addicted to alcohol and drugs and contemplates suicide before she and her newborn baby girl die from burns they receive in a hotel fire. Through the novel, Johnson realistically documents the pain, suffering, and economic constrictions of African American existence.[9]

8. Richard Wright, "Blueprint for Negro Writing," 36–40.
9. Richard Wright, "How 'Bigger' Was Born," xxxiii.

The philosophical and metaphysical dilemmas faced by Faith and Bigger are similar in many ways. Both characters are desperate, alienated from themselves and others, fearful, and victimized by their circumstances—mere objects manipulated by a grinding, oppressive, and largely impersonal fate. Both are seeking to overcome the brutal oppression they have faced at the hands of cruel and exploitative whites. Faith is searching for that something that will give her, as Bigger says, "that sense of fullness" that she knew as a child in Hatten County, Georgia, but it is nowhere to be found in the contemporary urban landscape of Bigger's Chicago.

That Johnson has considered *Native Son* is evident from his lengthy discussion of the novel in *Being and Race*. Johnson describes *Native Son* as a philosophical account of black urban experience through which Wrights asks, "What is it like to be thoroughly manipulated by others?" (*BR*, 13). Johnson discusses how skillfully Wright asks readers to interpret the world through Bigger's powerless and ultimately fated perspective, one "predestined for tragedy" (*BR*, 13). Similarly, Faith struggles against a host of opposition; her life, too, seems to be moving toward an unhappy end. Like Bigger, Faith's consciousness in the book is seared by her condition. She longs nostalgically for the rural past of her girlhood home and for the marvelous folktale stories woven for her by her father; yet these stories do not sustain her physically. Like Bigger, Faith longs "to merge [her]self with others and be a part of this world, to lose [her]self in it so [s]he could find [her]self."[10]

The realist story of Faith's struggles with her environment is set within a larger frame of oral storytelling. Johnson hints at his artistic strategy in "Being and Form," a chapter from *Being and Race*. In this chapter, Johnson challenges apprentice writers to open their horizons through variation. "As a playful phenomenological variation, try this: tell *Native Son* in the voice of the storyteller in my own novel *Faith and the Good Thing*" (*BR*, 48). As we will continue to discover, this is exactly what Johnson does. The narrator's voice works to put into perspective Faith's dilemmas and even distances the readers from it, since many times the narrator admits or hints at the stories' unbelievability and fictionality. Johnson uses the oral tradition to complete *Native Son*'s impetus while suppressing the social protest legacy of Wright's influential masterwork.

In his analysis of Ellison's intertextual revision of Wright's *Native Son* in *Invisible Man,* Gates writes, "By explicitly repeating and reversing key features of Wright's fictions, and by defining implicitly in the process of narration a sophisticated form more akin to Hurston's *Their Eyes*

10. Richard Wright, *Native Son,* 226.

Were Watching God, Ellison exposes naturalism to be merely a hardened convention of 'the Negro problem,' and perhaps part of the problem itself." In his incorporation of *Native Son* into his first novel, Johnson similarly exposes the limitations of Wright's naturalistic depiction of African American life. Instead of *reversing* or inverting, however, Johnson repeats, extends, and integrates *Native Son* and aspects of Wright's aesthetics into his novel. Following one of his central aesthetic principles of formalistic variation, Johnson immerses himself within the literary universe Wright's novel so powerfully affords, thereby incorporating and modifying Wright's influence.[11]

Johnson and Gardner

Adding another layer of complexity to the intertextual relationship between *Native Son* and *Faith and the Good Thing* is Johnson's close personal and professional relationship with John Gardner, who advised Johnson as he wrote *Faith and the Good Thing* and *Oxherding Tale,* and who had a tremendous influence on the development of Johnson's aesthetic. In a recent interview, Johnson referred to himself as "tabula rasa, without rigid preconceptions about literature" before meeting Gardner and becoming his apprentice. After writing six unpublished novels Johnson wanted the guidance of an experienced author, what he refers to as a "senior craftsman with greater experience than mine whom I could apprentice myself to." This led him to independent study with Gardner in 1972 at Southern Illinois University. Among Johnson's many artifacts from the relationship were letters from Gardner on the nature of art and Johnson's *Faith and the Good Thing* as he read it and offered suggestions. Johnson admired Gardner's "prodigious understanding of technique, his gift for voice and narrative ventriloquism, his magisterial, musical prose." Johnson points to Gardner as his premier mentor for developing an aesthetics dedicated to political and perceptual impartiality and openness. When Gardner died, Johnson lamented his passing in his journal, calling him a "giant of contemporary literature," and someone who saved him "six years of development . . . as a writer of philosophical fiction."[12]

Gardner's background in philosophy, his emphasis on genre crossing, precise craftsmanship and technique, and formalistic experimentation

11. Henry Louis Gates Jr. *Figures in Black,* 246.
12. Charles Johnson, "John Gardner as Mentor," 620–1; Charles Johnson, "Introduction to *On Writers and Writing,* vii–xxi; Johnson, "Where Fiction," 48; Charles Johnson, "Journal Entries on the Death of John Gardner," 270.

helped Johnson access new modes of formalist expression and leave behind strict naturalism and realism. According to Johnson, the post-sixties New Fictionalists "had found a way to make the practice of fiction interesting again after decades of naturalism." These writers included Gardner, John Barth, William Gass, Raymond Federman, and Ronald Sukenick, who had developed new techniques and strategies relating to narrative point of view for revisiting ancient literary forms, such as fables, parables, and tales. Especially important for Johnson's writing *Faith and the Good Thing* was the freedom to use the "tale-and-yarn telling tradition still close to the roots of oral storytelling."[13]

One of the central aspects of Johnson's aesthetic is the concept of formalistic virtuosity, an idea that can be directly traced to Gardner's nonrealist influence. Early in his career, Gardner published *The Forms of Fiction* (1962), an anthology of "older prose forms—yarn, sketch, fable, tale" because, according to Gardner, "I was sick to death of realism." From Gardner, Johnson inherited a reverence for ancient forms of literature and for a bent for encouraging writers to experiment playfully with those forms both as a way of opening up new creative possibilities and forms and as a way of commenting on the present through artistic vehicles from the past. As Johnson relates, Gardner believes that "much great fiction exploits the possibilities of 'genre-crossing,' or a cross-fertilization of one story form by another" (*BR*, 48–9).[14]

Johnson draws from phenomenology to further justify this formalistic integration or genre crossing. For, in crossing or blending genres—the oral narrative, the philosophical novel, the bildungsroman, and the picaresque as in *Faith and the Good Thing*, the artist momentarily inhabits another world (the aesthetic equivalent to phenomenology's "free variation") through the imagination, since every form or style, "impresses us as being a special interpretation of the world" (*BR*, 53).

In elucidating these points, Johnson brings the discussion back again to Wright, Johnson's other central literary forefather—he attacks Wright by saying that "men and women have written masterpieces with only a small bag of tricks" (*BR*, 53), including Wright, and closes the chapter by paying homage to writers who are able to create successful renditions of many different forms thereby creating new forms and new literary possibilities. In his ambivalence toward Wright, and his amalgamation of Wright and Gardner, Johnson is practicing his own form of aesthetic "cross-fertilization," as he plays his mentors against each other to create a kind of procreative synergy. In this context, *Faith and the Good Thing*

13. "Introduction to *On Writers*," xiv.
14. John Gardner, *On Writers and Writing*, 175.

becomes a combination of both influences and a conversion of both pushed toward new possibilities.

In addition to Gardner's formalist techniques, Johnson was attracted to many of Gardner's traditional aesthetic ideals that link art and morality. In *On Moral Fiction*, Gardner writes that art should address "the preservation of the world of gods and men," and states that "true art treats ideals, affirming and clarifying the Good, the True, and the Beautiful." These very words are repeated throughout *Faith and the Good Thing* in the narrator's rhetorical and playful questions, asking his audience, "Was it Good? Was it Beautiful?" In repeating these words Johnson has incorporated Gardner's traditional critical voice within the novel itself.[15]

Gardner applies the term moral to both the content and the style of the work of art. In clear opposition to the sixties and seventies postmodern trends of entropy and literary exhaustion, Gardner believes that art is humanity's salvation. If it is good art, it will have a "clear positive moral effect, presenting valid models for imitation, eternal verities worth keeping in mind" and stimulate moral action in its audience, as well as feelings of life-affirmation instead of cynicism and hopelessness. Art, in effect, is humanity's last stand against chaos. Yet, Gardner does not want to promote art that merely proselytizes. Throughout his writings Gardner, like Johnson, draws a distinction between art and propaganda. He states, "True art is *by its nature* moral. . . . It is not didactic because, instead of teaching by authority and force, it explores, open-mindedly, to learn what it should teach." Instead of preaching, true fiction "celebrates, compassionately suspending its moral outrage for the moment."[16]

Gardner's emphasis on morality in these terms affected *Faith and the Good Thing* and had a profound influence on Johnson's view of art. Part of the reason Johnson mourned his mentor's passing so much was Gardner's antagonist critical voice—"holding forth on our sins against civilized life and holding up art as a Way to redemption." In an interview Johnson stated that Gardner would chastise him for creating one-dimensional "straw-men" characters that Johnson only used to attack. This critique led Johnson to redefine his notion of socially responsible fiction: "I would like for people to look at my books and feel that they are socially responsible. I say that because I try my very best to be fair to every character on one level." For Johnson the novel that presented each character in a process of dynamic evolution and transformation "would be the ultimate moral fiction."[17]

15. John Gardner, *On Moral Fiction*, 16, 133.
16. Ibid., 18–9; Gardner, *On Writers*, 36.
17. Johnson, "John Gardner," 624; Little, "An Interview," 171–2.

Johnson tends to repeat Gardner's beliefs about artistic technique while questioning Gardner's moralistic certainty. In a reflection on Gardner's *On Moral Fiction,* Johnson argues that while Gardner "was our most inventive, prolific and controversial writer of serious fiction. . . . Unfortunately, Gardner's ideas on art cannot be systematically argued." Gardner's ideas are oversimplified, repetitive, and lacking in "critical compassion and sympathy." And, instead of arguing for a moral art, Johnson writes, "A 'moral fiction,' then, may do no more than rotate around various perspectives, treating each truth as if it were *the* truth (which it is for the character) and settle on no position at all." Finally, "We cannot say that some perceptions *should* take priority over others in fiction and still be on safe ground." Although Johnson was deeply influenced by Gardner, Johnson equivocates when it comes to demanding moral fiction. In his introduction to Gardner's collected essays, Johnson prefers the phrase *responsible fiction*; it is, he thinks, a less programmatic term.[18]

Despite Johnson's equivocations, Gardner's influence on *Faith and the Good Thing* was enormous, especially when read in the context of Johnson's dialogue with the tradition of African American literature. Johnson is quick to point out that Gardner praised *Faith and the Good Thing* for the "dignity" of the characters, "a characteristic he complained was missing in so many stories, all by acclaimed authors, who (he felt) wallowed in fashionable despair, entropy, defeatism, cheap fireworks, and a cynical vision of humankind." Gardner's editorial influence along these lines in some ways negated Johnson's ability as a former cartoonist to exaggerate and denigrate satirically. Also, it prevented Johnson from writing conventional Black Aesthetic social protest literature, a literature of sociological moral outrage, which urged exposing a social wrong through characterization, as in Wright's depiction of Mr. Dalton, the hypocrite who, on the one hand, mouths liberal platitudes while, on the other, he exploits poor blacks through his ownership of the run-down apartment building in the Chicago slum where Bigger and his family live.[19]

Gardner's influence on Johnson has clear ideological overtones. Johnson admired Gardner's knowledge of the classics and "his great love for fine storytelling regardless of the culture or race that produced it," seeing in Gardner a foil against the political battles that have divided university faculty in English departments during the culture wars. It is ironic that the path pointed out by his white traditionalist mentor leads Johnson back

18. Johnson, "Phenomenology of *On Moral Fiction,*" 148–53; "Introduction to *On Writers,*" xvi.
19. Johnson, "John Gardner," 620.

into the black vernacular tradition and African spirituality (albeit with a difference), a tradition already suggested in *Native Son* by its debilitating absence.[20]

The Novel

Faith and the Good Thing begins with Johnson drawing attention to the oral, folk frame of the narrative and the playful nature of the conjuring narrator, who magically recreates the well-known story of the girl on her quest for the good thing, for some kind of truth. The unidentified narrator recognizes that though this is a common oral history, handed down from generation to generation, it retains some essential qualities, such as Faith's beauty. It is a quintessential conjure or trickster tale, a verbal ritual told to affirm, empower, and preserve African American culture in the face of a hostile environment.

The plot begins with Lavidia, Faith's mother, dying. Although Lavidia seems driven by a joyless Western mechanistic view of the universe, she exhorts Faith to search for something else, some undefined good thing. The death of her mother radically alters Faith's philosophical perspective. At age eighteen Faith is orphaned and alone in the world. She seems displaced and alienated from her ordinary ways of seeing, and this compels her to search out meaning that will sustain her and reestablish her comfortable, life-affirming relationship with the world and its objects. Using a hybrid voice culled from a blend of Western philosophy and black folkloric tradition, Johnson's narrator speaks of Faith's quest for psychological and philosophical contentment and a sense of freedom after the disorienting loss of both her parents. Faith feels that the objects that surround her are "*out there,*" inaccessible, strange, and "charged-with-otherness." She is "no longer what she believed herself to be." She feels as though she is "drifting through a cold space filled with shadows" (*F*, 6).

Given the southern context of the story, the obvious avenue of comfort for Faith is her Christianity, especially since Lavidia was such a devoted churchgoer. But Faith does not find what she needs at the prayer meetings, in which the congregation members perform call and response. Self-doubts and feelings of discontent plague her, so that even though she calls, she is not moved by the experience, nor empowered by this southern African American vernacular tradition. The Reverend Alexander Magnus's message is ultimately a pessimistic one since he emphasizes in vehement Jonathan Edward jeremiads not to love the world and to confess

20. Gardner, "Introduction to *On Writers,*" xx.

sins. Juxtaposed to the reverend's flawed, Westernized, and ultimately destructive view of the world is, in Faith's mind, her father's alternative mythopoetic views, his "stunning fictions and well-meant lies" (*F*, 14).

Throughout the novel Johnson juxtaposes Big Todd's affirming and reassuring life philosophy against other, less complete philosophies, such as the harsh and abstract doctrines of sin and salvation in Faith's Christian church. Big Todd is essentially a romantic, one who believes in the possibilities of joining with a spirit in nature. In a classically romantic moment, and one that foreshadows many important passages in Johnson's later fiction, Faith experiences a liberating oneness with nature when she feels herself at one with the "heartbeat" of the universe: "And the grass and trees, it seemed, would bring their pulsations in line with them until the universe was a single heartbeat. . . . She felt herself at such times carried through the world as though she had wings, but not toward Glory, never toward Glory. Only back to earth, deep within its strange fabric" (*F*, 13). In this rapturous and mystical feeling of nature's presence, Faith recognizes the order and unity of existence.

It is through her memories of her childhood and of her father that Faith can temporarily reestablish the spiritual perspective that she misses, a spiritual perspective with striking similarities to the African religious worldview. According to this worldview, "all entities in the universe were otologically connected to each other at the deepest level of being through their connection with the Creator," whose original life force ran through all things. Indeed, "The natural order existed as a kind of complex machine powered by a *common* source of energy." The single heartbeat that Faith feels connected to is one that she has been separated from by her losses. For Faith, through the seemingly omniscient narrator, the happiest moments for her are the emotions recollected in tranquility; they serve also to throw the bereaved quality of her new condition into sharp relief. Big Todd gives Faith a "legacy of mythopoesis and love" (*F*, 15) that sustains her only intermittently during the duration of her search for the good thing. It is because of it, however, that she is compelled to keep searching, as her father had advised her, to find a more permanent peace and contentment.[21]

The Conjurer or Trickster

After her mother's death, Faith's inability to deal with her feelings of displacement, alienation, and despair lead her at the beginning of chapter two into the heart of African American southern culture, embodied by the

---

21. Roberts, *From Trickster*, 74.

mythical Swamp Woman. The Swamp Woman represents the antithesis of the Westernized Christian preachers in her Africanist spiritualism and magical powers. The novel's narrator connects her to part of the myth and folklore of the region and of slave culture, identifying her as a former spirit healer from Nubia before the coming of the European slave traders. As is characteristic of the trickster figure, the Swamp Woman is very much part of a communal belief system—she exists to exact revenge and to torment the white oppressors and to counteract their hegemonic power. As the empowered conjurer, she is famous for her forms of torment and revenge.

The Swamp Woman—and the novel—gains power from a central African myth of Kujichagulia and the Good Thing. When Faith arrives at the Swamp Woman's home, the Swamp Woman tells her a story about how the good thing was lost. Having the good thing, whatever it was, created a paradise on earth, which was destroyed by the questing Kujichagulia, who wants to analyze the good thing's essence. This motivation so angers the gods that they eventually hide it from him, and the world, forever, to prevent this kind of analysis, which focuses on the ultimate truth or essence. Interestingly, Kujichagulia's thirst to divine the essence of the good thing is replaced by his wife's more benign curiosity. Instead of needing to find the essence, his wife wants to experience the good thing and, in so doing, *becomes* the good thing through her quest. When the Swamp Woman reveals that she is Kujichagulia's wife, she tells how the gods rewarded her by giving her the power of a form-switching imagination. Although this novel is early in Johnson's career, such a denouement anticipates his later attacks on essentialist thinking, in whatever form it takes.

There is a further paradox. Although later in his career Johnson attacks the limitations and rigidity of the tenets of the Black Arts movement of the sixties, the Swamp Woman's character seems to embody some of the principles that helped to define that movement. In "The Black Arts Movement," Larry Neal writes that this movement "proposes a radical reordering of the [W]estern cultural aesthetic. It proposes a separate symbolism, mythology, critique, and iconology." In terms of ancient mythology, Neal means, "Spirit worship, Orishas, ancestors, African Gods, Syncretism/catholic voodoo, macumba." Through these primarily African spiritual vehicles Neal sees the possibility of solving the African American's problem of double-consciousness as identified by Du Bois, of feeling fragmented by the incompatibility of an African heritage and American citizenship. Neal writes of "The integral unity of culture, politics, and art. Spiritual. Despises alienation in the European sense. Art consciously committed; art addressed primarily to Black and Third World people." The revisionist thrust of black nationalism included a quest for a renewed sense of spirituality in opposition to the fragmentation and materialism of the Western worldview, one linked directly to the nourishing roots of African spiritual traditions. In its reliance on central African figures *Faith and the Good Thing* fulfills certain Black Aesthetic critical expectations, with, at the same time, an implied rejection of essentialist modes of thinking.[22]

The Beginnings of the Quest

Johnson dramatizes the central tension between African spirituality and dead Western rationalism through the metaphor of the bogs in which the Swamp Woman lives and creates. For Dr. Lynch, the scientist, life begins and ends in meaningless slime or algae, but for the Swamp Woman the same substance is procreative, abundant, and even aesthetic. While on the train to Chicago, Faith drifts into a dream about the Swamp Woman. She envisions herself as the Swamp Woman stirring her potion, which is depicted as an essential, beautiful, and ultimately mysterious life-substance. This water seems to be the source of her aesthetic power—it symbolizes the magic of her fluid imagination to adopt new shapes and to connect with the deepest mysteries of the past: "Often, at sundown, the water was as red as the blood of a calf—rich, opaque; then, at dawn, almost transparent enough for the bones of ancient beasts to be seen on its bottom" (*F*, 47). As is characteristic of Johnson's romantic views of the imagination's powers, not only does the bog water change in color and in texture, it is impervious to rational explanation and to examination, hiding more than it reveals, as if it is a symbol of the unconscious, and the mystery of artistic creation.

These moments of romantic rapture and reverie are offset by Faith's realist struggles as she battles against alternate philosophies and the harsh conditions of her environment and status as a poor young black woman. When she arrives in Chicago, where the Swamp Woman had told her to begin her search, she is brutally raped and robbed. Lying spread-eagle on the bed after the rape, Faith's consciousness is brilliantly rendered as she confronts the most traumatic and problematic aspects of her past, including the racist discrimination she suffered as a child and the racially motivated murder of her beloved father. This contemplative remembrance of her past spirals farther back—eventually she becomes one of her enslaved ancestors, forced to endure the horrors of the trans-Atlantic Middle Passage and the humiliation of being sold as property.

22. Larry Neal, "The Black Arts Movement," 272; Larry Neal, "Some Reflections on the Black Aesthetic," 13, 16.

Johnson does not allow Faith's memory to stop at enslavement. He takes her memories farther back in an act of imaginative archeology, returning to the very beginnings of humankind, connecting her to the development of the human race. "But that is not the beginning, not at all. Beneath her thoughts are more impressions, older ones of an ancient, eolithic world—a continent in the lush, tropical zone now sunken into the Indian Ocean" (*F*, 66). Faith pictures herself developing from half-human, half-animal until, over a period of centuries, her mind imposes an analytic order on the world, leading to scientific, technological discoveries that, apparently, led to the technology and practices of slavery, in which another human being is made into an "other," a commodity, capable of being bought and sold: "The brain itself and larynx and her body as a whole rushed to pace the development of the hand—to create man, society, and history; to build swift clippers and slave ships and manacles to make men, and especially women, the objects of desire; to weave the thick rope that stretched the strong neck of Todd Cross that hot spring day" (*F*, 66–7).

Even in this early hallucinatory passage, Johnson anticipates his treatments of slavery and philosophy in *Middle Passage*, when the links he forges between dualistic analytic thinking and slavery are seen very clearly. In some ways, Johnson's rendition of his familiar theme is made more powerfully in this passage, since its philosophical assumptions are less explicitly made than in *Middle Passage*, especially given the personal connection that Faith recognizes between slavery, technology, and the loss of her beloved father, who lost his life due to the implications of this dangerously flawed worldview.

In an echo of the forms in which Johnson is working, Johnson represents Faith's consciousness vacillating between the romantic and the realistic. Her moments of romantic reverie in the novel are indeed stylistic tour de force, since in them Johnson represents historical time as circular rather than linear—through Faith's tortured hallucination he spirals back through time to show the connectedness and interrelatedness of all humans, powerfully implying the inhumanity of separating one human from another, defining some as different. In this particular example, Faith is linked with the lynching death of her own father by virtue of her connectedness to the rest of humanity and its development. She is connected to that death because she is part of the ancient heartbeat that connects all of humanity through a single rhythm, a rhythm that was disrupted by a dangerously flawed philosophical perspective. This provocative example stands alone in African American literature in its evocation of a mystical connectedness between the victimizers and the victimized of the slave-chattel system. In this and other passages in the novel, early indications of Johnson's integrationist vision emerge, thwarting the expected ideological messages that would usually accompany an art informed by African traditions and heritage; it is the philosophical fictive equivalent of his comic strategies to shock, to create disjuncture, and to offer fresh interpretations of experience. In this early novel, Johnson demonstrates his belief that fiction is a philosophical enterprise that allows for a penetrating archeology of meaning.

Faith's Nadir

Like Maggie in Stephen Crane's masterful naturalist novel *Maggie: A Girl of the Streets*, Faith, alone and penniless in the city, is forced to support herself as a prostitute. In so doing, Faith surrenders to mens' gender stereotypes—she becomes a mere sexual object, with no individuality or hope for her condition. She "accepted her bondage" (*F,* 69) and succumbed to the pressures of "a personal history over which she had no control" (*F,* 70). She seems to yield to a pessimistic and despairing worldview at this point in her quest, losing her father's romantic legacy of mythopoesis and love. She seems destined, at this point in the novel, to end up like Maggie, who dies an ignominious, anonymous death, perhaps drowned in the East River by a menacing client.

Increasingly desperate and unhappy, Faith attends a storefront church. Instead of finding salvation within, however, she finds only doubt and a strong memory of her childhood minister's crisis of belief, which reflects her own lack of faith. She realizes more than ever that emptiness pervades the world and her inner self, and she decides, because of this, to grasp onto the objects of material comfort as her Good Thing. Accompanying this resignation to the world of material objects is Faith's recognition that she is running out of the oral histories she uses to entertain her clients. Paradoxically, it is through art, or storytelling, that Faith maintains some semblance of power within her dehumanized status as a prostitute. When this impulse goes, so too goes Faith's resolve to find the Good Thing that will bring some sense of reassurance and a liberating joy.

Faith's despair seems to call forth her soul mate in the novel, Dr. Richard Barrett. Barrett is a former Princeton professor who robbed Faith after she arrived in Chicago. Barrett's life has been destroyed by his unyielding search for the Good Thing and the greatest good. He, like Kujichagulia, leaves his wife, children, and everything that is important to him to pursue truth. And, like Kujichagulia, Barrett's wife also pursues the Good Thing, yet without his fixation on discovering one central truth. Barrett is different from his wife since "she was never tortured by beauty—she never looked at a rose and, by dint of reason, went beyond it to yearn for roseness" (*F*, 93). Significantly, the book that Barrett is obsessed with completing—the *Doomsday Book*—is blank, revealing the poverty of his philosophical perspective in his essentialist search for the single truth, for roseness. Yet, he is a complex character, since his belief that it is the search for the Good Thing that gives life meaning anticipates the Swamp Woman's wisdom at the end of the novel, a wisdom that Faith will eventually inherit and accept. Despite his flawed perspective, Barrett embodies some of the novel's central themes. He confesses, for instance, that, for him, the "entire world was allegory for me. . . . It always pointed beyond, or perhaps below, itself to something more good, more real and glorious than what I could see" (*F*, 93). What he calls this central "exegesis of the rose, of the world" (*F*, 93) is his life's philosophical work. His is an essentially religious and romantic perspective: he believes that there is a greater presence that inhabits the universe and can be read in the material. As a crazed and self-destructive believer in that which cannot be seen, Barrett's vision is a primary one in the novel since it hints at the presence of something transcendental beyond the material—to an empowering mystical and spiritual divinity.

Unlike the Swamp Woman, Barrett has no creative outlet, no means to uncover this realm of allegorical meaning. His book, or his artistic product, remains blank. Into this blankness, Faith conjures a primarily romantic vision of her childhood. While viewing it she realizes it is "a sort of screen onto which her thoughts spread out like an oil slick on the surface of the sea" (*F*, 94). Into this blankness, Faith recalls "the particular magic and music of a world" which for her now is very far removed from her present harsh day-to-day reality (*F*, 95). Barrett's philosophical life exegesis remains unrecorded and undocumented, unmythologized and finally incomplete. Although he sees himself as a didactic poem, he is unfinished perhaps because his meaning is lost to everyone but Faith, his questing companion, a like-minded soul, who remains haunted by his image after his sudden death on a Chicago park bench.

Barrett, the wise and doomed idealist romantic philosopher, is juxtaposed with Issac Maxwell, who is himself Faith's next stage in her search for the Good Thing. Maxwell represents a kind of Hobbesian capitalist materialism—a survival of the fittest defined by those with the strongest wills and the most money. As can be expected given Johnson's ideological and philosophical predispositions, Faith's identification with Maxwell and his competitive, materialistic, middle-class lifestyle represent her failure and weakness of will. In marrying Maxwell, Faith settles for mere survival and comfort, the opposite of Barrett's spiritually noble, albeit flawed quest. She accepts pretense and a life of appearances as a way to endure. She submits to making herself a wife-object for Maxwell, succumbing to defeat in "this twirling exchange for supremacy of wills" (*F*, 107).[23]

Throughout the middle space of the novel Johnson keeps the unresolved tension between the competing philosophical perspectives always in the foreground. Even while she is living with Maxwell, Barrett's image constantly haunts her, reminding her of her own surrender, self-betrayals, and forgotten quest. His image appears several times in Faith's mirrors until her eyes are drawn to the picture window, signaling her transition into the "dead living," as opposed to the vibrant and powerful "living dead" exemplified by Swamp Woman and Big Todd's inspirational legacy. The narrator defines the "dead living" as purely mechanistic beings, without souls or depth. In this state Faith becomes a spiritually empty physical shell.

Competing Aesthetics

Faith's way out comes in the form of Alpha Omega Holmes, a boyfriend from childhood, who represents the beginning and ending of her quest and the truth she has forgotten—the life-affirming aesthetic vision embodied by her father. Coincidentally, Holmes becomes a subject for one of Maxwell's journalistic interviews on black ex-cons and visits their house. Holmes embodies the black folk spirit. As a writer, Maxwell wants Holmes to fit into his expectations of the disenfranchised and disgruntled oppressed black victim—showing more rage and angry protest-oriented willpower. Instead, Holmes is more interested in telling stories and jokes that resemble, in many ways, Johnson's own cartoon one-liners, such as the joke about the summer that was so dry the bullfrogs forgot how to swim.

Johnson uses this contrast between Holmes and Maxwell to comment on and react against the Black Aesthetic and perhaps to anticipate the stereotypical black cultural nationalist critical reaction to *Faith and the Good Thing*. Where Maxwell (and the black cultural national critic) wants realism, rage, and a kind of social determinism for his newspaper article, Holmes gives him instead a kind of dreamy fairy tale sentimentality. Holmes is the alternative allegorical artist, countering Maxwell's demands for naturalistic racial outrage and gritty urban realism.

---

23. This novel contains an unsympathetic view of marriage as predominately social pretense. Johnson's later novels end instead with the promise of marriage and long-term domesticity as the answer to the central philosophical quests.

Holmes's aesthetic, however, is not as limited or sentimentalized as Maxwell would have it. Through his art Holmes achieves a problematic isolating modernist solitude and a romantic narcissism. The walls of his apartment are filled with charcoal sketches that "revealed not poverty but a sort of voluntary retreat from the world" (*F*, 145). Revealingly, Holmes's aesthetic is portrayed with more sympathy than is given Maxwell's hardened realistic perspective. In comparison with Holmes's apartment, Faith's apartment is bereft of spiritual meaning.

Johnson privileges Holmes's perspective by linking Holmes explicitly to the Swamp Woman and the narrator, who are storytellers like Holmes, capable of lying, but lying well and entertainingly. He is, like her father, "Someone strong, a giant, a Great Fool among frightened ones, a weaver of words and delicious little lies to woo other people and live by" (*F*, 153). It is, after all, Holmes's narrating and storytelling power that attracts Faith. Holmes reminds her of the power that she herself once possessed, but lost due to her mistaken belief in materialism and Maxwell's perspective. Unlike Barrett and Faith, Holmes is able to translate and transcend his philosophical and spiritual searchings into art—the Swamp Woman's portrait dominates his apartment murals. He often tells Faith that she needs to "seize the day,"—the very same motto that adorns her father's tombstone.

The sexual encounter between Holmes and Faith is a metaphor for Johnson's belief in the unifying powers of art, the possibilities of imaginative variation, and the pursuit of the transcendence of relativism. In their sexual union, Holmes "projected the image of himself in her, as she did within him until they seemed to exist, not as two people, but as one" (*F*, 154). Divisions of gender are overcome in this moment, "the moment their images melted, drifted, and were transformed" (*F*, 154). Faith reconsiders her identity. No longer an isolated being, she feels as if she were transformed into the mathematical principle of AOH:FC (a combination of their initials), exemplifying Johnson's own integrationist aesthetic on an intimate personal scale. In this moment of sexual rapture, both characters are able to transcend the limitations of their relativist perspectives to become something else. This is exactly the power of the conjurer, who is able to inhabit other selves, other perspectives through the mysterious power of the intersubjective aesthetic vision.

The Mystical Aesthetic

Johnson uses a discussion of Holmes's aesthetic to further comment on the limitations of realist art. Holmes is endowed with Big Todd's spontaneity, wisdom, and connection to African American folk culture; and through her union with Holmes, Faith finally realizes one of the Swamp Woman's truths, that the good things are ephemeral. Faith watches Holmes conjuring on his canvas and meditates on his technique. Holmes is not concerned with mimesis or realist verisimilitude; he has "no truck with describing the scene. Instead, Faith reflects, "He was . . . calling these things, changing, twisting, and transforming them into—what? Order" (*F*, 158). His sense of aesthetic order and control come from his feelings and his desire to become, like the Swamp Woman, the ultimate life artist, who does not need a canvas on which to create. Holmes says, "She didn't need no paints, or stone, or sheet music, and I swear I believe she could change herself into any damn thing she pleased" (*F*, 159). Although Holmes has not reached this level yet, he is closer than anyone else in the novel so far to achieving personal happiness and his own Good Thing, since he can conjure meaning and artistic expression. It is as if with each new character, Johnson brings his readers closer to a philosophical and aesthetic position more in accordance with his own.

Faith and the Good Thing recreates a realist narrative until the end, when Faith's experience in Chicago comes full circle and she dies with Holmes's unwanted child after a fire in the very same hotel where she had first been raped. Had Johnson ended the novel there, in the grim flames, he would have recreated the pessimistic determinism of Stephen Crane's novel and have shown the triumph of fate and environmental factors over his main character. Even in her moment of physical death, however, Faith enters into the realm of magic, supernaturalism, and myth that Johnson provides for her as an antidote to her oppressive conditions. As the killing flames surround her and her baby, a wall mural seems to spring to life, and Faith sees her father in the shape of a tree: "tall, slender, eternal: Big Todd" (*F*, 178). Her father encourages her, looks forward to her rebirth into nature's life-force. In a touching response to her father's vision, she longs, as did Holmes, to become "merged, so to speak, with the canvas itself" (*F*, 157). Holmes is unsuccessful, but Faith becomes part of her imagined canvas—the picture of her imagined childhood and the legacy of mythopoesis and love left to her by her father.

In the nonrealist denouement, Johnson opens up the magical possibilities of fiction and has Faith rising up from her hospital bed to, comically, ride the train from Chicago back to Georgia. As a ghost Faith circles back to where she started her quest by visiting the Swamp Woman. The Swamp Woman, or Imani, offers Faith the central truth revealed by the gods. The gods had given her a sign that lights up the sky: "In This Sign Conjure" (*F*, 191). Thus Imani, the Swamp Woman, became a conjurer, "invokin' spirits from sweet-gum trees, dredgin' up demons from the most common things of all" (*F*, 191). Conjuring—the ability to create and to tell stories and to inhabit new worlds and beings—is revealed as the Good Thing. Unlike dead analytic scientific rational method or empiricism, conjurin' or creating calls forth what is left out of dualistic empiricism—love.

In her explanation of the Good Thing, the Swamp Woman recites some of the central tenets of African spirituality, critiquing the Western "Age of Reason," for its "lack of intimacy with the world" (*F*, 192). Since Faith still does not understand what the Swamp Woman is talking about, the Swamp Woman gives her a demonstration. She asks Faith to look outside, and to Faith is revealed the unity of nature, and the soothing presence of her father, whom she sees in one of the tallest elm trees. Through this romantic epiphany, in which she experiences unity with nature, Faith moves to the next level, the stage of the spiritual trickster and conjurer. She becomes Imani by stepping into her skin, fulfilling the role of sacred interpreter, able to "spell out the cosmic designs in human language," and to disclose "how the human mind and heart are themselves epiphanies of a calmly transcendent sacredness."[24]

Faith as the Swamp Woman is magically polymorphic. In creating such a liminal, transcendent, and playful figure, Johnson offers his rendition of the African trickster and conjuring character to advance his own brand of phenomenological insight. Instead of remaining locked in any one identity, Faith is made to realize that she has the opportunity to sample many different identities and gather a synthetic wisdom from differing perspectives. She finally defines aesthetic and personal responsibility as "factoring the possible number of paths to the Good Thing, but not becoming fixed, or held to those paths in her history, or the history of the race" (*F*, 195). This is the novel's central dialectical message. Responsibility for conjurin' includes the responsibility of phenomenology's imaginative or self-transcendence and the importance of remaining, as an artist and philosopher, open to new experience. Johnson's final statement concerning the importance of remaining flexible and open represents a significant ideological and aesthetic statement. Not only does it reverse the Black Aesthetic imperatives of holding to a specific and particularistic racial identity and history for purposes of empowerment, it also undermines any approach that emphasizes a fixed racial heritage or tradition, as does Baker's blues matrix and Gates's theory of the intertextual vernacular as self-contained approaches. Instead, Johnson's assertion, even at this very early stage of his literary career, emphasizes how the particular can lead

24. Roberts, *The Trickster*, 234, 3.

to the universal and to a transcendence of self and race. Despite Wright's integrationist aesthetics, such a choice transforms the legacy of *Native Son* from a protest novel into a philosophical novel that concerns itself more with aesthetics and creativity than with politics.

Although written years before the publication of *Being and Race*, *Faith and the Good Thing* becomes the exemplar of the kind of intersubjective role-playing that the writer of serious fiction must master. Johnson writes that through the process of "losing himself in the rich interpretative material provided by others" like an actor has immeasurable benefits since "this kind of writer is forever obliged to obliterate for the duration of his fiction his own pettiness, to surrender his prejudices in order to seize another's way of seeing, then faithfully present it in the story" (*BR*, 45). Through Faith, Johnson is faithful to this aesthetic criteria; this aesthetic of eclecticism and willed intersubjectivity has moral implications, both reflecting and refuting Gardner's beliefs about art. In Johnson's review of Gardner's *On Moral Fiction*, he writes that "the social payoff" of only emphasizing black victimization as "*the* truth" is "immoral, . . . particularly when it smothers all others in a fiction (or life)." In writing *Faith and the Good Thing*, Johnson has reversed generic and ideological expectations associated with sociologically oriented black protest fiction.[25]

In its ostensibly apolitical and certainly anti-revolutionary denouement, *Faith and the Good Thing* reflects Gardner's interpretation of Herman Melville's "Bartelby the Scrivener" in "Bartelby and Social Commitment," included in the volume of Gardner's essays introduced by Johnson. Gardner reads into this story a drama of art versus reality. Bartelby, who has been denied freedom, justice, and mercy in life, finds salvation through death, through art. Gardner writes that art offers freedom and opportunity not available in life. Bartelby, through the narrator's act of storytelling "is now transmogrified to eternal life in art"; "Bartelby the Scrivener" is essentially a Christian story of individual transcendence and redemption. Similarly, Faith, in the end, is transmogrified through art (the oral storyteller's narrative) into an empowered eternal life. Yet, in a correction of Gardner's certainty about moral fiction, through Faith, Johnson emphasizes how there is no one perspective that takes precedence over all others. She does not discover the central truth; rather, she looks to the future to find new paths of knowledge. Faith is Johnson's corrective answer to Black Aestheticians *and* to his mentor John Gardner.[26]

25. Johnson, "Phenomenology of *On Moral Fiction*," 155.
26. Gardner, *On Writers*, 12.

Faith and the Good Thing and *Native Son*

In contrast to Faith's final liberated state, Bigger's sense of wholeness and empowerment after the murders is fleeting. In his prison cell he is anguished by his fear of death, ambivalence toward his white Marxist lawyer's admonitions, and feelings of guilt and responsibility toward his family. Like Faith before she becomes the Swamp Woman, Bigger longs for a sense of unity with others. Echoing Wright's statements of the need for a sense of wholeness for African American writers and artists, Bigger becomes an artist figure longing for expression and a feeling of comforting interconnectedness. In his dark jail cell, Bigger holds out his hands and imagines that they are electric wires powered by the electric battery in his heart. He fantasizes about communication across time and space through electricity to touch other hearts: "And in that touch, response of recognition, there would be union, identity; there would be a supporting oneness, a wholeness which had been denied him all his life." Like the characters in *Faith and the Good Thing* who are not artists, Bigger ends the novel wishing for a way to communicate and to extend the feelings of wholeness, unity, and connection with others that he felt only imperfectly in his murderous acts of creation. In the above quote Wright turns the death-imagery of the electric chair into a life-giving and life-affirming electric charge of expressive communication, able to create a mystical wholeness and communion and overcome the walls that separate African Americans from each other and from whites. It is a dramatization of his integrationist hopes as expressed in "The Literature of the Negro in the United States," where he writes optimistically about the future of race relations and technology in America, "We stand at the crossroads. We watch each new procession. The *hot wires* [emphasis added] carry urgent appeals. Print compels us. Voices are speaking. Men are moving! And we shall be with them." Such a possibility is only hinted at in *Native Son*. By suggesting an alternative, Wright reveals his romantic tendencies, especially since the possibilities for cross-cultural and interracial unity are so tragically denied and half-imagined.[27]

Because of Wright's perspective, Bigger longs for "a vast configuration of images and symbols whose magic and power could lift him up" and help him transcend his position as a second-class citizen alienated from the rich intensity and rewards of being a truly liberated human being. He longs for conjuring power that would sustain him and give him the same

27. Wright, *Native Son,* 335; Richard Wright, "The Literature of the Negro in the United States," 147.

hope Faith has discovered to conquer death and the inevitability of racist discrimination. Yet *Native Son* is dominated by images of artistic powerlessness and longing. Bigger cannot express his feelings through writing, speaking, or the "hot wires" of mass media. Tragically, Bigger ends the novel voiceless, misunderstood, and conflicted, fully aware that his life is over "without anything being settled, without conflicting impulses being resolved." Although critics have made much of Bigger's final acceptance of responsibility and seeming peace, his voice is "full of frenzied anguish." The "ring of steel against steel" is the powerful and unforgettable aural image that ends the novel. *Native Son* ends with a brilliant prophecy of impending racial violence and revolutionary insurgency. Unlike Faith, Bigger is denied transcendental aesthetic empowerment and a potentially liberating reconnection with his heritage.[28]

Faith as the Swamp Woman fulfills Bigger's artistic longings, turning her death into a victory through the very folkloric forms that Wright hoped would disappear into the mainstream of American literary expression. She overcomes death and is liberated from the racist and socioeconomic restrictions of her environment through her magical, shape-shifting powers. Able to project an endless array of images and symbols onto the world, Faith has become an otherworldly force, historicized and engendered by Africanist beliefs, certainly, yet free to move out of any particular racial or historical identity. Faith becomes the ultimate liminal trickster figure by breaking down the boundaries between the human and non-human, between the oppression she suffered under in her state of human bondage and thinghood. In the end, Faith looks forward to assuming new identities, new roles, and finding in them the dialectical, cumulative truth that each offers. She will continue to pursue different paths as the liberated artist figure might, imaginatively projecting herself into the subjectivity of another following the dictates of phenomenology's principle of imaginative variation or, a kind of formalistic virtuosity, yet without the need for the tools of artistic production. She becomes a potent life-artist, living her art.

Deeply informed by the Black Aesthetic's promotion of African forms and figures, *Faith and the Good Thing* shows Johnson diffusing the expected or even anticipated revolutionary message, substituting or replacing liberatory aesthetics where the ideological payoff should be. *Faith and the Good Thing* is not a politically useful book in ways that would be recognized by the Black Aesthetic critic. Faith does not become, for example, solely a revolutionary force. In ways that conform with his satiric

---

28. Wright, *Native Son,* 256, 382, 392.

vision and artistic production as a cartoonist, Johnson highlights the free-play of artistic discovery over explicit political relevance or application (i.e., the dicta of artistic utility).

Faith is also a nascent figure for integrationism in her polymorphic and finally synthetic identity since she will always *look* for another path or identity to inhabit or conjoin with as a shape-shifting conjurer. Johnson's efforts to free himself from the ideological realm are therefore only partially successful, given the inherent ideological implications of his aesthetic and his characterization.

However, in writing *Faith and the Good Thing,* Johnson completes a playful phenomenological novelistic variation in taking poignant sub-themes from *Native Son* and Wright's criticism—aesthetic and integrationist longing—by extending and fulfilling them. Although *Faith and the Good Thing* lacks the dramatic narrative urgency of *Native Son,* in part due to its lengthy philosophical digressions, it stands as a significant statement of Johnson's earliest attempt to define his aesthetics through fiction and to forge a revised philosophical and ideological vision while making the transition to literary art.

Writing *Faith and the Good Thing* allowed Johnson to find his own voice by including and then breaking the spell of naturalism's powerful stylistic influence. There were still issues, however, that this novel did not address, "despite these satisfactions, I *still* had not *dealt* head-on with the matters closest to my heart and mind." In an interview, Johnson states that he was not satisfied with *Faith and the Good Thing.* "I realized I hadn't pushed intellectually in terms of my own interests or artistically in terms of the things I wanted to experiment with as far as I possibly could." *Faith and the Good Thing,* while neither as accomplished nor as expansive as Johnson's next novel, *Oxherding Tale,* establishes Johnson's affinity with African spiritualism and further illuminates his complexly ambivalent relationship with the Black Aesthetic. *Oxherding Tale* takes the next step in tentatively exploring the social implications of his aesthetic and his subsequent break with Gardner's influence. In these and other ways, Johnson's first novel anticipates *Oxherding Tale*'s stunning achievement.[29]

29. Johnson, "Introduction to *Oxherding Tale,*" xiii; Little, "Interviews," 1.

3

Social Duty

Hinduism, Zen, and the
Art of *Oxherding Tale*

Between 1974 and 1982, Johnson wrote and repeatedly revised a novel that incorporated his interests in Eastern religions and spirituality, especially Zen Buddhism. *Oxherding Tale* takes the more implicit religious impulse of *Faith and the Good Thing* and converts it into an explicit statement of spiritual exploration and affirmation. In the novel, Johnson modifies Zen's prompt to withdraw from society with Hinduism's concern for social duty and communal responsibility. Using both Eastern religions, Johnson furthers his integrationist position and begins to explore what will become the central theme of his next novel, *Middle Passage*—the spiritual nature of human community.

In a December 1974 letter to John Gardner, Johnson discusses writing *Oxherding Tale* and the difficulties of promoting the social side of Zen:

> I'll plunge back into *Ox-Herding Tale* until it's finished, hoping—as I go along—that I can convince my reader (and you) that certain aspects of the Zen Buddhist vision are social. As we said, this is tricky, and the philosophy can't be taken in its entirety because it doesn't say, for example, that we should tackle problems as a community, by joining hands after seeing a performance of Greek tragedy. In fact, it leads men *from* society; but I think it leads them back again, not merely to the society of man, but the wider society that includes all sentient things: animals, plants, the universe as a whole. More important than that, it's [*sic*] essential message is selflessness [in] an absolute sense, sensing beauty in all things, because, in its odd, quirky vision, every moment of history and immediate input of the universe is reflected in everything.

80

Johnson's mystical and romantic aestheticism merges here with his social ideals into a well-integrated whole. His assimilative vision is here undeniably religious in its connection between Zen epistemology and the aesthetics of the interfusion of man and nature. *Oxherding Tale,* completed eight years after he wrote this letter, takes the first steps toward fulfilling his initial motivation. This study's conclusion will show how a more recent short story, "The Work of the World," completes the connection Johnson makes between aesthetics, Eastern religions, and human community.[1]

Johnson refers to writing *Oxherding Tale* as one of the major challenges of his artistic career. Its difficulty was directly related to his ideological purposes; Johnson wanted "to create a work of philosophically challenging fiction" in a decade "when the work of black male writers was systematically down-played and ignored in commercial New York publishing." He points out that critics praised it for its move away from gender and racial victimization. *Oxherding Tale* came out in the same year as Alice Walker's *The Color Purple.* Johnson reflects on this connection, adding, "I'll leave it to readers to decide which book pushes harder at the boundaries of invention, and inhabits most confidently the space where fiction and philosophy meet." Whereas in *Faith and the Good Thing,* Johnson utilizes aspects of African religious heritage to inform his novel, in *Oxherding Tale,* Johnson sets Eastern and African religious traditions within the context of slaveholding nineteenth-century America to challenge publishing trends and critical expectations.[2]

Another difficulty in writing the novel was Johnson's departure from Gardner's thinking. His further movement away from Gardner's mentorship is evident in his introduction to *Oxherding Tale* and in interviews. Johnson relates that Gardner seemed puzzled by *Oxherding Tale* and that "I remember one of the things he said very specifically. We were having an argument at his house . . . and I was talking philosophy and Buddhism and John just said, 'Buddhism's wrong.' He was very Protestant." It was with *Oxherding Tale* that Johnson began his divergence from Gardner to pursue another line of thinking about cultural identity and the African American self when filtered through the lens of Eastern philosophy. Despite their disagreements, Johnson's journal entries written at the time of Gardner's death, and later published, show he wanted to discuss the finished product with Gardner since "it would have been a way to extend our often heated

---

1. Charles Johnson, "Letters to John Gardner," 5–6.
2. Johnson, "Introduction to *Oxherding Tale,*" ix–xix.

conversations through the mails on the nature of selfhood and (black) identity."[3]

Oxherding Tale is courageous in its revolutionary fusion of differing influences and creative examination of African American identity. It is the perfect embodiment of Johnson's additive and integrationist aesthetic, in which all is contained, and nothing lost. The novel works on several levels and appropriates the metaphysical and developmental underpinnings of the slave narrative, which, in the words of Houston Baker, addresses "the problem of being itself." In Frederick Douglass's narrative of his life, for example, "in the lettered utteranced is assertion of identity and in identity there is freedom—freedom from slavery, freedom from ignorance, freedom from nonbeing, freedom even from time." Similarly, Johnson's narrator gathers and records an identity that counters his condition of non-being as a chattel slave. Despite its ambitious and radical departure from Western sources and the predominately Christian narrative of conversion that helps to define the nineteenth-century slave narrative as a genre, *Oxherding Tale* follows a familiar passage from bondage to emancipation.[4]

The quest journey documented in *Oxherding Tale*, despite its structural similarity to the slave narrative, is unlike any other depicted in American literature. It is truly a fresh variation on African American identity and history, creatively fusing the philosophical insight of two complementary Eastern religious traditions—Zen and Hinduism—to underscore the personal and communal rewards of individual enlightenment and liberation. In it Johnson takes a step away from the isolated, even narcissistic liberation that Faith experiences at the end of her journey from metaphysical bondage to freedom.

Ten Oxherding Pictures

Also unlike *Faith and the Good Thing*, which heavily relies on Wright's influence, *Oxherding Tale* relies primarily on a twelfth-century Chinese Zen Buddhist parable, *Ten Oxherding Pictures*, to provide the primary intertextual catalyst. In *Ten Oxherding Pictures*, which is verse accompanied by drawings produced in the fifteenth century, Chinese Zen master Ka-ku-an Shi-en charts the steps that the oxherder takes to spiritual liberation and enlightenment. The interplay between Johnson's novel and these

3. Little, "Interviews," 5; Johnson, "Journal Entries," 271.

4. Houston Baker Jr., "Autobiographical Acts and the Voice of the Southern Slave," 245; James Olney, " 'I Was Born': Slave Narratives, Their Status as Autobiography and as Literature," 157.

drawings demonstrates again Johnson's commitment to and fascination with visual art; a fascination that dominates his aesthetic. Using sequential panels, *Ten Oxherding Pictures* depicts a spiritual quest as the oxherder tries to discover his true identity, or true self. The ten drawings show the oxherder seeking the ox, finding the ox, catching and taming the ox, and then riding the ox home, where both ox and self are forgotten in a flash of enlightenment. After being enlightened, the oxherder is transformed into a spiritual healer, entering the marketplace dispensing bliss and enlightenment with the touch of his fingertips.[5]

In his 1991 National Book Award acceptance speech, Johnson reflects on how *Ten Oxherding Pictures* influenced his novel: "And I came across the ten Zen Buddhist Oxherding Pictures, by Kakuan Shien (twelfth century), and those drawings fascinated me. . . . They show a young herdsman who feels his ox—which is a Chinese symbol for the self—has been lost. And so he's looking for the ox, the self." Johnson wished to create both a novel that would take advantage of the parable's insights and a "slave narrative that in its progress paralleled the 'Ten Oxherding Pictures.'" Throughout the novel, Johnson's narrator, Andrew Hawkins, born a slave, seeks spiritual, psychological, and physical emancipation. The slave narrative and Zen spiritual quest have much in common, since, as Zen scholar D. T. Suzuki comments, "The whole system of Zen discipline may thus be said to be nothing but a series of attempts to set us absolutely free from all forms of bondage." Like Kaku-an's oxherder, Andrew goes through many steps or stages for attaining liberation. Yet, the conclusions of the two narratives are somewhat different, and they show, simultaneously, Johnson's inclusion and modification of his Zen source.[6]

The liberation that the oxherder in Kaku-an's parable achieves is vintage Zen. After seven frames, the herdsman finally catches and tames the ox, and the narrative climaxes in the stunning eighth frame, "The Ox and the

5. William Gleason, "The Liberation of Perception: Charles Johnson's *Oxherding Tale*," 705–28. Gleason does an excellent and profound job of exploring Johnson's use of Kaku-an Shi-en's *Ten Oxherding Pictures*. While I agree with much of Gleason's analysis, I reach different conclusions. For instance, Gleason argues that "the Zen parable literally helps write Johnson's narrative." Gleason charts exact similarities and inversions between the novel and the Zen source. My argument, on the other hand, emphasizes how Johnson takes general ideas from *Ten Oxherding Pictures* and fuses them with other spiritual traditions, such as Hinduism, to serve his own evolving ideological and aesthetic beliefs.

6. Charles Johnson, "The Philosopher and the American Novel," 12; Johnson, "Introduction to *Oxherding Tale*," xiii; Daisetz Teitaro Suzuki, *The Zen Doctrine of No Mind*, 27.

Man Both Gone Out of Sight," which depicts nothing but an empty circle. Kaku-an comments, "All is empty—the whip, the rope, the man, and the ox: / Who can ever survey the vastness of heaven?" The oxherder disappears since "there exists no form of dualism," nor even the concept of the self. It is the moment of enlightenment: "When this state of things obtains, manifest is the spirit of the ancient master." The oxherder, in finding his self, has realized its ultimate emptiness. In his commentary on *Ten Oxherding Pictures*, Lex Hixon summarizes Buddhist philosophy, "In Buddhist teaching, our intrinsic nature is revealed to be that we have no intrinsic nature, that is, the essence of our consciousness is void, free, or open. The dimensions of Enlightenment suggested by these ten pictures become progressively more comprehensive as this essence of consciousness, or what Zen masters call our *True Nature* becomes clearer and clearer."[7]

The emptiness or *sunyata* doctrine in Buddhism is a complex one, yet it is important for understanding the dialogue of aesthetics and community in *Oxherding Tale*. Buddhism stresses that everything, including the self, is marked by impermanence and change. Instead of a fixed, identifiable self, Buddhists see a "collection of rapidly changing and interacting mental and physical processes" that point instead to "not-self" or "no-self." Buddhism implies that "no such self-existent substance exists: the world is a web of fluxing, inter-dependent, baseless phenomena." According to the Buddhist four holy truths, believing in an "I" or self is one of the reasons for attachment and suffering: The not-self encourages people to examine their selves and through that process to see that everything is, indeed, not-self, "thereby destroying all attachment and attaining *Nibbana* [Nirvana]." The ultimate goal of Buddhism is to transcend individual craving: "*Nibbana* is only attained when there is total non-attachment and letting go." Nirvana, meaning "extinction" or "quenching" is often described in Buddhist scripture in negative terms: the unborn, the unbecome, the unmade, the deathless; yet, "*Nibbana* is also seen as 'emptiness' (*sunyata*) . . . in that it is empty of attachment, hatred and delusion, being known in this aspect by deep insight into phenomena as 'empty' of a substantial self."[8]

Paradoxically, Zen meditation aims, therefore, at a state of "no-mindfulness," or "no-thought" to reflect this state of "no-self." Harvey writes, "In Zen practice, when mindfulness reaches high intensity, it is seen as so taken up with its objects that it is not aware of itself, so it is

7. Daisetz Teitaro Suzuki, *Manual of Zen Buddhism*, 133; Lex Hixon, *Coming Home*, 60–1.
8. Harvey, *Introduction to Buddhism*, 52–100.

'no-mindfulness.' " In this state of consciousness carefully attuned to the present moment, the mind is free from thought; it is aiming toward the moment of enlightenment, in which there is a sudden realization. "It is a blissful realization where a person's inner nature, the originally pure mind, is directly known as an illuminating emptiness," which connects it to the emptiness of heaven and earth. Thus, when Kaku-an's oxherder reaches the eighth frame, he has realized the inherent emptiness of self and the universe, which is a vision of unity.[9]

Elaborating on the meaning of the "no-self" or "no-mind" Zen Buddhist doctrines, D. T. Suzuki quotes ancient Zen master Ta-chu Hui-hai. "When a mind, thoroughly understanding the emptiness of all things, faces forms, it at once realizes their emptiness. With it emptiness is there all the time, whether it faces forms or not, whether it discourses or not, whether it discriminates or not. Why is it so? Because all things in their self-nature are empty; and wherever we go we find this emptiness. As all is empty, no attachment takes place." The enlightened being, the *Bodhisattva*, "knows how to make Use of emptiness, and thereby he attains the Ultimate." The *Bodhisattva* and *Arahat* figures have attained a nirvanic experience in life and are thus worthy of respect. He or she has "attained complete mental health," has "seen through the delusion of a permanent self or I," and has attained the seven factors of enlightenment, including vigor, joy, tranquillity, concentration, and equanimity. He or she is aware that there is no-self and so is unafraid of death. To the *Bodhisattva,* "the sky and the palm of his hand were the same to his mind."[10]

Certainly Kaku-an's *Ten Oxherding Pictures* is the quintessential Zen Buddhist text. After the stunning eighth frame, which represents the sudden flash of inspired enlightenment, the oxherder, aware of the unifying emptiness of all forms, is given a glimpse of the essential rhythm of the universe. In the ninth frame, "Returning to the Origin, Back to the Source," which depicts the empty circle quietly filled with a nature scene of mountain and asymmetrical tree, the oxherder "watches the growth of things, while himself abiding in the immovable serenity of non-assertion. He does not identify himself with the maya-like transformations [that are going on about him], nor has he any use of himself [which is artificiality]. The waters are blue, the mountains are green; sitting alone, he observes things undergoing change." As Hixon comments, "Enlightenment simply *is* the blue lake and the green mountain."[11]

9. Ibid., 272–5.
10. Suzuki, *Zen Doctrine,* 49; Harvey, *Introduction to Buddhism,* 64–5.
11. Suzuki, *Manual of Zen,* 134; Hixon, *Coming Home,* 79.

In the final frame, "Entering the City with Bliss-Bestowing Hands," the oxherder, drawn larger than life and towering over a village dweller, returns to the city and his home as a magical spiritual figure. He associates with the townsfolk in the center of town, and suddenly they are converted into Buddhas: "Bare-chested and bare-footed, he comes into the market-place; / Daubed with mud and ashes, how broadly he smiles! / There is no need for the miraculous power of the gods, For he touches, and lo! the dead trees are in full bloom." The oxherder now personifies awakened enlightenment. Instead of turning his back on the world or transcending earthly life, the transformed oxherder returns to ordinary human existence to help others attain what he has found. His enlightenment has not separated him from humanity; it has made him aware of his connectedness. He has found his true nature to be total compassion, perfect nonviolence, and unwavering truthfulness.[12]

Although the oxherder returned to the city and common humanity, he is hardly a mundane or ordinary figure. In addition to his supernatural powers and his larger-than-life appearance, there is something mysterious and cryptic about him. In the commentary on the tenth frame, Kaku-an writes, "No glimpses of his inner life are to be caught; for he goes on his own way without following the steps of the ancient sages." He is the curious Zen devotee, at once supremely individualistic, private, and yet connected with all life-forms. Kaku-an's narrative stresses his difference and removal from society. His "thatched cottage gate is closed, and even the wisest know him not."[13]

In his *Oxherding Tale,* Johnson modifies this tendency toward Zen self-removal and supernaturalism found in the Kaku-an text through a fusion with Hinduism's four stages of life, stages that emphasize one's obligation to society and maintenance of the social order while on the path to spiritual release or liberation. For the upper-caste males, the first two stages of life are the student and the householder, in which "the individual is supposed to study the sacred scriptures and learn sacred rites that uphold the world and to marry, procreate, and serve society by means of his caste *dharma* [social duty]." The final two stages, forest dweller and world renouncer, involve retirement from the world, in which "a man leaves his family, gives up his social roles, and retires to the forest to meditate."[14]

The Hindu conception of *dharma* is important for a discussion of *Oxherding Tale* since, near the end of the novel, Andrew states, "my

12. Suzuki, *Manual of Zen,* 134; Lex Hixon, *Coming Home,* 89.
13. Suzuki, *Manual of Zen,* 134.
14. David R. Kinsley, *Hinduism: A Cultural Perspective,* 94.

dharma, such as it was, was that of the householder" (*OT,* 147). *Dharma,* meaning duty, law, righteousness, or moral merit, "connotes religious and social duties; that which one ought to perform by virtue of the place one occupies in the social order . . . the concept of *dharma* is thus articulated in terms of one's station in life, since this ideally expresses the level of one's development as a spiritual being." In the householder stage of life, in which one marries, works, has children, and pursues spiritual development, one must realize that one's duty, or *dharma,* is not only to oneself, but also to the wider community. *Dharma* "involves an awareness of one's dependence upon others and the consequent recognition that one must adjust one's needs and desires to those of others; that one must work for the good of all as well as for oneself." Although the resolution of the novel is somewhat truncated and oblique, Andrew's harmonious marriage and stable social situation point to his successful adoption of the role of householder, in which he, as a prosperous family man and socially responsible citizen, upholds individual and community ideals and, by so doing, perpetuates the social order—a somewhat surprising outcome for a former slave. Certainly by the end of the novel, Andrew resembles the Hindu model of the householder more than Kaku-an's supernatural, larger-than-life, reclusive, and enigmatic Zen spiritual figure.[15]

Thus Johnson's *Oxherding Tale* is a complex, idiosyncratic mixture of Hinduism and Zen Buddhism. That this exotic blend of influences and beliefs is brought to bear on the spiritual and psychological life of an escaped slave in mid-nineteenth-century America is an intriguing and provocative commentary not only on history, but also on contemporary racial identity and individual contentment. Through this esoteric and exotic novel, Johnson works through the empowering possibilities of his own cosmic imagination as it rummages through diverse spiritual traditions and transposes them onto a bildungsroman, the Western narrative of self-improvement and education. By deploying Hindu and Zen epistemologies, Johnson in many ways transcends the historical circumstances of slavery to concentrate on using his novel as a vehicle for spiritual allegory.

Oxherding Tale

The novel starts with a one-liner comic premise reminiscent of Johnson's early cartoons. Set in the antebellum South, *Oxherding Tale* begins with Andrew Hawkins's retrospective *Tristram Shandy*-like account of his origins, which involves his father, George, and George's owner, Jonathan

15. Eliot Deutsch, *The Bhagavad Gita,* 8.

Polkinghorne. Late one night, after many bottles of madeira, Jonathan suggests that he and George trade places for one night and sleep with each others' wives. When Anna Polkinghorne discovers she has had sex with a slave, she kicks George out, and the two men pass each other when they are running back to their respective beds. This visually oriented comic scene could easily be the subject of one of Johnson's cartoons. Because of his origins, in this improbable night, Andrew is at home nowhere, popular in neither the white nor the black world. Suffocated by slavery and eager for his freedom, Andrew, when a young man, works out an agreement with Jonathan Polkinghorne to work for a year to earn enough money to return and buy his family and Minty, another slave whom he has known since childhood.

Johnson wrote romantic reveries for Faith in *Faith and the Good Thing*, and he uses a similar technique in *Oxherding Tale*. Johnson revisits Andrew's education in transcendentalism and philosophy through flashbacks. The romantic connection with nature is echoed in his reflections on his education with Ezekiel Sykes-Withers, a transcendentalist and mystic who tutors Andrew in Greek, philosophy, music, and Oriental thought. When walking with his tutor by the river, Andrew feels "strangely, that each smell, each sound was sheer magic—that he and I, these frothy waves, this dust seamed wind were somehow essential for the world to be, as if [they] were full of some queer godstuff" (*OT*, 31–32). In this state of rapture Andrew glimpses the kind of spiritual unity that he will experience in full at the end of the narrative as a free man. In these moments Andrew senses "an intimation of my freedom—my *real* freedom—ordering these objects now into love, now into beauty" (*OT*, 32). Accompanying Andrew's physical manumission will be the shape-shifting powers of the life-artist in the tradition of the Swamp Woman. Before attaining this aesthetic freedom and power, Andrew must first find and tame his ox, his self. His first step is to leave the plantation of Cripplegate and begin his apprenticeship with Flo Hatfield.

Andrew's Education in the Senses

In chapter three, "In the Service of the Senses," Johnson draws from Hermann Hesse's *Siddhartha*. A fictional rendition of the life of the Buddha, *Siddhartha* shows the main character leaving the luxury of his father's estate to become a *samana*, wandering ascetic. After years of living this life of sensory denial, Siddhartha becomes an apprentice to a courtesan and dallies in sensual experience. Kamala, the courtesan, is described as having "a bright red mouth like a freshly cut fig." Flo Hatfield is described in similar terms as a primarily sexual object. She is a "sumptuous woman with a little red mouth" (*OT*, 37). In Hesse's novel, Siddhartha "learns the games of love" from Kamala: "She played with Siddhartha for a long time, repulsed him, overwhelmed him, conquered him, rejoiced at her mastery, until he was overcome and lay at her side." In a comic inversion of Siddhartha's education, Andrew's experience makes him feel he is enrolled in a course on voluptuous sensuality. He learns that the lover of Flo has to be polymorphous and play different roles, including characters from different literary genres: the romance, the sea story, the Arthurian legend, and the Eastern parable. Andrew's apprenticeship is literary and spiritual as he strives to overcome the limitations of his previous condition.[16]

An anomaly among nineteenth-century women, Flo is a spiritual artist of the senses; she represents one of the many paths to truth that Andrew will follow in the novel. Flo, like Kamala in *Siddhartha*, believes that the body is a vehicle to the spiritual self, a way to enlightenment. In order to participate in this way, Andrew must dedicate himself to Flo's teachings and try to eliminate his own needs and desires. Like Siddhartha, however, Andrew quickly recognizes the limitations of the path and wearies of it. After nearly a year in the service of Flo, Andrew longs for more meaning than Flo can offer him. He realizes that she is merely a male fantasy and that they are both imprisoned by their devotion to their senses.

Andrew's discontent over his status grows. He realizes that Flo has no intention of paying him money for his apprenticeship, and he resents her position as sovereign of Leviathan, where African Americans are viewed as nothing more than physical creatures, devoid of intellect, emotions, and imagination. The status to which his bondage relegates him rankles the philosophic Andrew. About slavery he especially resents the fact that "it created a long, lurid dream of multiplicity and separateness," and that it "epidermalized Being. The Negro—one Negro at Leviathan—was needed as a meaning" (*OT*, 52). In an article addressing perceptions of the black body, Johnson defines epidermalization as a phenomenological process of white stereotyping whereby whites perceive African Americans only as exteriors, defined only by their skin color and their bodies. This caricature comes freighted with negative overtones of stained skin, which "recalls

16. Hermann Hesse, *Siddhartha*, 51, 72. In his recent article, "*Oxherding Tale* and *Siddhartha:* Philosophy, Fiction, and the Emergence of a Hidden Tradition," Rudoph P. Byrd carefully explicates the relationship between the two novels, stating, "Indeed, it is not an exaggeration to assert that *Siddhartha*, in the conceptualization of *Oxherding Tale*, occupies a position of co-equality with *Ten Oxherding Pictures* by Kaku-an Shi-en, a foundational work of Zen Buddhism, and the conversion and slave narrative of American and African American literature," 550.

defilement, guilt, sin, [and] corpses that contaminate," and denies the African American individual an imagination and intellect. When reduced by epidermalization, the black person has lost control of his self: "Our body responds totally to this abrupt epidermalization; consciousness for the subject is violently emptied of content; one, in fact, draws a 'blank,' though clearly for the white Other my interiority is, if not invisible, a space filled with sensuality, crime, or childlike simplicity." It is exactly this intentional stereotyping that Andrew seeks to avoid in Flo's rigidly defined and metaphoric body-state, which reduces its slaves to a source of physical labor.[17]

The Zen Aesthetic

To break out of this mode of epidermalized and reductive being, Andrew attacks Flo. Ironically, he uses physical force to end his apprenticeship. To avoid working in the mines and becoming further enmeshed in mere physical existence, Andrew flees north. He escapes with another bondsman, Reb, the coffin maker and veterinarian at Leviathan, and the two men pass for white. Reb is a mysterious figure, descended from a magical African tribe, the Allmuseri, a tribe that figures prominently in *Middle Passage*; he represents the way of the truly enlightened figure in its pure, unadulterated form. The great-grandson of a powerful *osuo*, or leader, Reb is trained in the spiritual, magical, and aesthetic practices of this mystical tribe. Not only does he learn the formulas for making medicine, rainmaking, and charms from various tribes, he also learns how to project himself into the lives of other objects, animate and inanimate, through the magic of his imagination. Andrew reflects on Reb's powers: "It took up ten thousand hosts, this I, slipped into men, women, giraffes, gibbering monkeys, perished, pilgrimaged in the animal and spirit worlds, and dwelled peacefully in baobab trees. He learned intimately the life of these objects and others, died their unrecorded deaths, and ever returned to himself richer, ready to assume a sorcerer's role" (*OT*, 49–50). Like Faith's ability, Reb's conjuring power allows him, through the power of his imagination, to inhabit any form.

This form-switching imaginative ability is a central feature of Johnson's aesthetic. In *Being and Race,* Johnson writes that the ability of the artist to achieve a transcendence of self to "surrender his prejudices in order to seize another's way of seeing" (*BR*, 45) is the central feature of philosophical fiction because it opens up the possibilities for seizing on human variation

17. Johnson, "Phenomenology of the Black Body," 597–98.

and the diversity of experience. Meditating on this magical ability of art as a pathway for self-transcendence and unity, Johnson asks, "What are the possibilities of being human, the parameters, the indefinite, individual variations onto which our lives open? Fiction, in a funny Buddhist sense, might even be called a Way" (*BR*, 45). Like the artist, the polymorphic Reb returns to himself after these magical flights of intersubjective knowledge wiser, informed by the power of the serious artistic process of creation. At its most ambitiously eclectic, the character Reb embodies Johnson's deeply held aesthetic strategy of imaginative variation.

Like the Swamp Woman and the conjurin' narrator of *Faith and the Good Thing,* Reb is a talented storyteller. He tells his stories to Andrew. In Reb's conjuring, Andrew learns of the dramatic Middle Passage and of Reb's role on board the *Fortunata* as singer and "the shaper of gentle songs" (*OT*, 50) for the captured Allmuseri members. In Reb's story-telling Andrew follows the history of the Allmuseri and the experience of imprisonment in Cuba's holding camps. While Reb is named three different names by three different whites, his spirit remains untouched, undamaged. Reb's magical conjuring powers and direct Allmuseri heritage protect him, even during the horrific traumas of enslavement.

Reb's Allmuseri lineage and spiritual knowledge closely resemble Buddhism's selfless philosophy. Reb's superhuman denial of his own desires resembles the elevated *Bodhisattva*'s quenching of the fires of attachment and desire. As Andrew reflects, "Reward he did not expect. Nor pleasure. Desire was painful. Duty was everything" (*OT*, 76–7). Reb's strenuous path to enlightenment is a "Way of strength and spiritual heroism . . . dead to hope" (*OT*, 76–7). Andrew refers to Reb as a "Never-Returner," (*OT*, 147) a reference to Buddhism's belief in "Non-Returners," those holy persons who "ha[ve] destroyed even subtle sensuous desire and ill-will, so that great equanimity is the tone of his experience, and [they] cannot be reborn in the sense-desire world." The emptiness that the *Bodhisattva* understands, ironically, serves to connect him or her with others, since all are empty and, thus, there is no difference between them. As part of his spiritual perfection, the *Bodhisattva* works to help and to teach others; the *Bodhisattva* has "reconciled wisdom with compassion."[18]

Reb's own movement from enslavement to perceptual and spiritual emancipation precedes the narrative present of *Oxherding Tale,* yet Johnson recalls it to parallel and foreshadow aspects of Andrew's development. Just as Reb overcomes despair after the deaths of his wife and daughter,

18. Harvey, *Introduction to Buddhism,* 65, 71, 121.

Andrew will have to overcome despair after the deaths of Minty, his first love, and his father. After Reb's wife dies, his daughter begins to show symptoms of pellagra, a terminal disease. In desperation, he turns to begging for money for medical treatment. Through this humiliating and unsuccessful process, Reb learns that he can only survive if he surrenders to what happens to him and accepts it. After that moment of Zen enlightenment and "no-self" realization—similar to that of Kaku-an's oxherder— Reb receives some money, only to discover that his daughter had already died. After that day he devotes himself to a disciplined life of self-denial and sacrifice.

Despite his inability to achieve Reb's nearly superhuman spiritual perfection, Andrew recognizes Reb's Zen aesthetic and metaphysic as an effective subversion of and rebellion against slavery. In a new world that denies blacks selfhood, Reb has constructed a strategy of absorbing suffering and misfortune, of living in the moment, of being "dead to hope," and, at the same time, achieving liberation. Additionally, Reb's ability to project himself into others allows him to anticipate their every move and outsmart them. Reb's Zen way of selflessness and strength later allows Reb to defeat the allegorical slave-hunting Soulcatcher, Horace Bannon. Although Andrew does not and cannot follow Reb's way, he does, as we will soon discuss, benefit from his example.

When Andrew asks Reb about his casket-carving technique, Reb's answer radiates Zen Buddhism's preoccupation with emptiness and eliminating egoism, equating it with purified aesthetic process. He tries to eliminate the influence of his rational mind and memory of carving techniques. He engages in a time-consuming process of forgetting and self-nihilation until the answer reveals itself to him. These rigorous techniques of forgetting and self-emptying offer an intriguing enactment of Johnson's aesthetic as expressed in the final pages of *Being and Race*. Just as Schopenhauer wrote that everyone "must stand before a picture as before a prince, waiting to see whether it will speak," Johnson says that a literary critic and writer must practice what he calls "egoless listening" (*BR*, 123). This kind of listening is the necessary precursor to a more individualistic and diversified African American fiction, unbound from the precedents of the past, relying only on individual experience. Yet, as with Johnson's own integrative aesthetic, the Schopenhauer quote shows Johnson's dependency on (visual) art—allowing art to speak through the individual artist and stimulate artistic production. In Reb's Zen selflessness, Johnson has embodied his ideas for a "Reb"ellious African American literary tradition, beholden to no one perspective. Paradoxically, part of *Oxerherding Tale*'s embedded aesthetic philosophy stresses individualism through Eastern holism in its emphasis on the individual's idiosyncratic way of seeing as an artist.

Reb's aesthetics are taken from a central parable from the "Inner Chapters" of Chuang Tsu's writing, a fourth-century B.C.E. Chinese Taoist. These influential chapters show Chuang Tsu "anticipating Zen Buddhism and laying the metaphysical foundation for a state of emptiness of ego transcendence." In this exchange, Prince Wen Hui's cook talks about his aesthetic techniques in carving an ox. Prince Wen Hui admires his cook's skill and mastery of his art. The cook tells the prince that "when I first began to cut up oxen, I saw nothing but oxen. After three years of practicing, I no longer saw the ox as a whole. I now work with my spirit, not with my eyes. My senses stop functioning and my spirit takes over." This egoless reduction to quiescence is mirrored in Reb's artistic process; in both one must discard the self before starting to create. Additionally, this Zen strategy is similar to phenomenology's central principle of *epoche*, which calls for the elimination of all presuppositions before apprehending or experiencing an object.[19]

Phenomenology and Zen

Johnson uses Reb the artist and aesthetician not only to explore a strenuous Zen aesthetic, but also to merge aspects of phenomenology and Zen. This idiosyncratic blend is seen in the novel's most dense and compelling symbol of Andrew's "self"—Reb's multisided carving of Andrew, which begins as an uncarved block.

Andrew's misunderstanding of the block as it nears completion demonstrates the distance he must still travel at this point in the narrative to his own liberation and understanding of his true nature. His description of the unconventional sculpture is dominated by puzzlement and incomprehension. The first side only bears his likeness while the other sides are more enigmatic in their meaning. Andrew's interpretation of this paneled sequential narrative emphasizes his need for realism; he is disappointed that only the first side looks like him. He can recognize his likeness, since as ingenue, he is still smoothly unmarked and unstained by white perception and epidermalization. In the opening visual art panel, his trials and tribulations have not yet left their mark on him.

With his knife, Reb anticipates Andrew's future in the second panel, which is, according to Buddhist's emphasis on suffering, the future of every human, a predictable mixture of suffering and joy. It depicts a curious

19. Gia-Fu Feng and Jane English, *Chuang Tsu: The Inner Chapters,* vii, 55.

figure, "someone else," whose expression is "a worldly blend of ecstasy and pain, sickness and satiation" (*OT*, 77). The third side is even stranger to Andrew since it portrays a (white) master with solid ties to the community. Although this is exactly what Andrew becomes through his decision to pass for white and marry the daughter of a prominent white doctor, it is not something he can foresee. Using his projective intersubjective aesthetic, Reb foreshadows Andrew's fate, reconstituting conceptions of linear time into a circular pictorial sequence.

Significantly, the fourth side is blank. This side is the most intriguing because it breaks the pattern of sequential visual art narrative. Although Andrew is at a loss to explain this panel, there are several symbolic possibilities. If one reads the figurine as an evolving narrative, the fourth panel could represent the ultimate stage in Zen spiritual unfoldment or development—self-annihilation, or the liberating loss of self. In this context of the neo-nineteenth-century slave narrative, it could foreshadow Andrew's final stage, in which he, seemingly, has transcended the boundaries of race and heritage by passing for white. Certainly, the final "frame" could represent Kaku-an's stunning eighth frame of the empty circle, symbolizing the stage in which "All is empty." Yet, this is curious if this sculpture is meant to correspond to Andrew's development, since he, unlike Reb or Kaku-an's oxherder, never achieves the goal of total self-effacement or self-nihilation. Instead, the fourth side would seem to represent the unfinished nature of Andrew's identity, its unwritten future possibilities, which directly involves Andrew as audience as he participates in constructing the meaning of the art work to fill its absence.

This intriguing four-sided figurine can be interpreted as the embodiment of Johnson's philosophical method. In an interview, Johnson explains that in the phenomenological method, "Things are given to us in profiles. Sides, angles, but not the entire thing. . . . That is much like where we find Andrew Hawkins and certainly Rutherford Calhoun at the ends of *Oxherding Tale* and *Middle Passage*." Through the lens of Andrew's misreadings, the fourth side, then, can take on yet another meaning: one can interpret this final blank profile as an expression of Reb's Zen aesthetic and as a metaphoric indication of Johnson's wish to keep the possibilities for artistic expression phenomenologically ever-open and in-process. The fourth panel is, after all, "where one mounted this odd figurine" (*OT*, 77). On another, more self-reflexive level, Johnson's inclusion of the blank fourth panel may represent his desire to break away from the rigidity and limitations of cartooning or drawing into the more multisided medium of writing. Perhaps as a nod to the nothingness doctrine in Buddhism, Johnson resists concluding or explaining fully

Reb's mysterious paneled narrative. Whether the narrative is empty or full depends, therefore, on the reader's cultural perspective.[20]

Also self-reflexively, Johnson explores his pervasive aesthetic's more dangerous features through Horace Bannon, the murderous bounty hunter and slave catcher, who perverts Reb's and, ultimately, Johnson's strategies for unethical, even immoral purposes. Bannon has very strict aesthetic laws that he describes for Reb and Andrew when they are making their escape north into the white world by traveling at night. Around a campfire, Bannon explains his techniques that allow him to catch and kill runaway slaves. Bannon's techniques are explained in aesthetic terms. Just as Reb projects himself into his subjects to complete his aesthetic project, so, too, does Bannon. Bannon explains his successful techniques: "You *become* a Negro by lettin' yoself see what he sees, feel what he feels, want what he wants" (*OT*, 115). Thus the subject's desire for respectability makes him easy prey for Bannon. It is when the bondsman loses hope of attaining his desire that Bannon is able to complete his mission. And, as we will see, being "dead to hope" is different from being "hopeless."

Bannon's aesthetic laws and Zen Buddhist-inspired techniques have never failed. Bannon's face is an eerie amalgam of features of his African American victims. Bannon is the monstrous "racial mongrel" (*OT*, 67) who graphically represents interracial and intercultural mixture gone awry, uncontrolled by moral or religious principles. As Andrew only learns in his last meeting with Bannon (in the novel's closing pages), his father, George Hawkins, was one of Bannon's victims. This explains why, when Andrew first meets Bannon at Leviathan, he sees in Bannon a resemblance to his father. Hawkins's features have been grotesquely incorporated or integrated into Bannon's own. Unlike the more positive representations of intercultural unity and integration that emerge in *Middle Passage* and even at the conclusion of *Oxherding Tale*, Bannon's portrait reveals the monstrous aspect of Johnson's preferred aesthetic and how it can potentially lead to a collation of profiles that is only hideous and, finally, evil—an insight that foreshadows the pervasively pessimistic mood of his short story collection, *The Sorcerer's Apprentice*.

The Black Aesthetic

Where Reb had countered racism and chattel status with Zen self-abnegation, George Hawkins counters the denial of self with a simplistic

---

20. Little, "An Interview," 163.

and defensive reversal of white values, a reversal that ultimately is self-destructive. After his expulsion from Jonathan and Anna's home, George thinks of whites as devils and is strongly committed to the historical mission of racial uplift. The character and his actions serve as a link within the story to the sixties' Black Power movement and black cultural nationalism. However, there are echoes of the parodic stance of Johnson's cartoons in Andrew's response. He calls George's rhetoric a "mantra of cliches." Johnson parodies black cultural nationalist ideology through George's characterization: "Grief was the grillwork—the emotional grid—through which George Hawkins sifted and sorted events, simplified a world so over-rich in sense it outstripped him"(*OT*, 142). Johnson's correction (through Andrew) of this perceptual deprivation or limitation points toward a reintegration with the whole of humanity from which this ideological excess has segregated him. This self-imposed misery does not just limit George's ability to perceive the richness of phenomena and nature, it eventually kills him. His despair calls forth the Soulcatcher, making his death more suicide than murder.

In a striking parallel that echoes the vocabulary used to describe George's limitations, Johnson, in *Being and Race,* criticizes the Black Aesthetic. However well intentioned or necessary, doctrines such as Negritude or Cultural Nationalism shut off "the free investigation of phenomena" (*BR*, 26) and run the risk of calcifying perception for the African American artist. Johnson uses extreme analogies to illustrate his points, comparing it to fascist art in Germany during the 1930s and criticizing the black artist who adopts it since it represents "a retreat from ambiguity," and the realization that black history "must be seen as an ensemble of experiences and documents . . . capable of inexhaustible readings" (*BR*, 20). In the allegory of aesthetics that dominates *Oxherding Tale,* Johnson takes a similarly negative view toward George Hawkins's perceptions of the world. Instead of using his fictional rendition of his critical complaints to reject totally the Black Power movement and its powerful legacy, however, Johnson demonstrates through Andrew's quest how it is an integral part of a contemporary African American identity. As he progresses in his quest, Andrew becomes a compilation of all that has gone before, not necessarily in an exclusive way.

Metafiction and the Slave Narrative

In one of two metafictional and self-conscious asides in the novel, "On the Nature of Slave Narratives," Johnson changes the narrative voice from

Andrew's first person to an authorial first person. He leaves his characters still journeying northward to make some self-reflexive comments about the slave narrative form. This essayist interlude is significant not because of what it says about slave narrative form and the movement in the novel from bondage to liberation but because of its identification of the slave narrative as an evolutionary form, which gathers its meaning from its historical precedents, "No form, I should note, *loses* its ancestry; rather, these meanings accumulate in layers of tissue as the form evolves" (*OT,* 119). In his quest for liberation, the now displaced and secondary narrator, Andrew, is a mere symbol of phenomenological and aesthetic process. As narrator, he is a combination of the conventions inherited from the slave narrative (first-person narrator recounting education and movement to liberation), the novel of manners (his cultured eighteenth-century voice addresses the reader as "Sir"), the picaresque (loosely related adventures forming the plot and inclusion of a partner, the use of humor), and the philosophical novel (the open discussion of philosophical positions).

In the second aside, entitled "The Manumission of First-Person Viewpoint," Johnson further investigates the conventions of the slave narrative, especially those relating to point of view. Johnson's third-person narrator seeks to liberate *Oxherding Tale* from the invariant feature of slave narrative form: first-person viewpoint. Instead of switching viewpoints from first to third, for example, Johnson's narrator wants to redefine Andrew's self: "The Self, this perceiving Subject who puffs on and on, is, for all purposes, a palimpsest, interwoven with everything—literally everything—that can be thought or felt" (*OT,* 152). Through the slave narrator, who, as reporter/writer, constructs and renders the fictional world, comes the principle of the "first-person (if you wish) universal" (*OT,* 153). These statements dramatize Johnson's basic phenomenological and Zen Buddhist beliefs that individual perceivers both contain everything through their perception and are responsible for everything as the authors of their own inclusive beings. Thus even Johnson's modifications of the narrative point of view are informed by his spiritual beliefs.

Thinly Veiled Autobiography

When Andrew finally ends his problematic middle passage as he moves from the black to the white world, he settles in Spartanburg, a small town in Pennsylvania. There he adopts an appropriately Spartan lifestyle as the novice spiritual seeker passing for white and constructs for himself, in true Ben Franklin fashion, a new identity. Andrew profits from the dazzling education received from his tutor by becoming the town's new schoolteacher, replacing Evelyn Pomeroy, whom Johnson has included in the novel to further elucidate his aesthetic beliefs.

Through Pomeroy, Johnson explicitly lays bare some of his central ideas about fiction. In tracing the arc of Pomeroy's history, Peggy reveals to Andrew that in her first story, written when she was only six, Evelyn wrote about an unloved white girl who transforms suddenly into an African American boy, a plot device that inverts the central storyline of *Oxherding Tale,* in which a Negro boy, Andrew, who is unloved, wakes up one morning as a white man. Happy to be relieved of her teaching duties, Evelyn leaves town. She later writes to Andrew from New York, where she is completing her novel. Complaining about the "sterility" of contemporary fiction, she believes that a novel should be a well-plotted "experiential feast, a three-ring circus of humor, suspense, ideas and images, a whole world of people tied together by *plot*" (*OT,* 130). Such an ambitious and antiminimalist position perfectly blends with Johnson's own literary ambitions and achievement, which so often blend humor, plot, and allegory into an ambitious fusion. Through Evelyn's pronouncements, Johnson shows his antagonism toward the tradition of the plotless metafictional anti-novel pioneered by the Surfictionalists of the sixties and, at the same time, toward the reigning aesthetic principles of rigorous postmodern fiction, which also call into question the viability of plot and character.

Not only does Pomeroy rehearse Johnson's aesthetics—ironically within a metafictional aside—Johnson has invested her with *his* history as a writer in his movement from the Black Aesthetic protest novel to a more self-determined voice. After publishing, like Johnson, a critically acclaimed first novel at twenty-six, she cannot finish her second novel, just as Johnson struggled for six years to finish his, *Oxherding Tale,* after *Faith and the Good Thing* was published. Pomeroy, "constitutionally, a romantic writer" (*OT,* 143), was at first deeply influenced by Harriet Beecher Stowe's *Uncle Tom's Cabin.* Her close intertextual relationship with this influential precedent, however, grows problematic when she mimics the novel by writing her own protest novel and realizes that she hates Stowe's novel and her own efforts because of her romantic sensibilities. This split with and dismissal of *Uncle Tom's Cabin* resembles Johnson's own inclusion and transformation of *Native Son* and other influential protest novels. As discussed in the first two chapters, Johnson confronts the novel and finds his own voice through *Faith* after six apprentice novels.

Liberation (Almost)

Andrew finds personal contentment through marriage to Peggy Undercliff, the scholarly daughter of the town doctor. Peggy is a revision of the Flo Hatfield character. Instead of seeing Peggy as an erotic object, Andrew perceives her more fully. His adventures and exposure to different philosophical positions have altered his perspective. Andrew's male gaze has moved inward to see Peggy's inner beauty, her intellectual gifts, and her sense of irony. By this point in the novel, Andrew has overcome the constraints and limitations imposed on him earlier by his masculine ego, an ego that warped his view of women, like Flo Hatfield, into primarily sexual objects.

Although reluctant to get married, Andrew is blackmailed into it by Dr. Undercliff (as Rutherford is almost blackmailed into marriage at the beginning of *Middle Passage*), who uncovers Andrew's past and threatens to expose him unless he marries his daughter. The wedding, however, is a transcendent moment, a moment that is reminiscent of Faith and Alpha Omega Holmes's sexual union in *Faith and the Good Thing* during which "their images melted, drifted, and were transformed" (*F*, 154), that stunning moment in which their individual egos and identities were overcome. Andrew and Isadora felt "translated" into "some parallel world, where the absences of life were presences, the failures here triumphs there, a realm of changeless meaning for which the only portal was surrender" (*OT*, 140). It is as if Christian, Buddhist, Platonic, and Hindu conceptions of transcendence and otherworldly presence intersect in the chapel where "that light rippled . . . like Platonic *nous* emanating from the One" (*OT*, 140); they have become a sacred representation of black-white integrationism, of interracial amalgamation and the spiritual release from the confines and boundaries of race and individual identity. Their mutual identity is deeply informed by the Buddhist concept of surrendering individuality in favor of a more holistic identity. Together Andrew and his wife reject individual desire and construct their life on "what we built in the interstices" (*OT*, 145).

After this marriage ceremony, Andrew discovers, much to his surprise, that he is above all a family man, a householder, committed to his wife and to the community. Although Andrew's psychological development is not resolved at this point, the novel comes to a spiritual conclusion with Andrew's symbolic union with another person through love. As a procreative couple, they seek to uphold the order and balance of the world—the first social duty, or *dharma*, of the Hindu householder: "After the war, Fruity and I turned to the business of rebuilding, with our daughter Anna (all is conserved: all), the world" (*OT,* 176). Through Andrew's domestic bliss Johnson thus revises Zen's (and Reb's) strenuous ascetic individualism into a more community-oriented denouement that reflects Hinduism's concern with service, duty, and sacrifice.

The novel's conclusion, infused by Eastern thought, reverses and revises the tradition of doomed interracial marriages in African American fiction evident in such novels as Frank Webb's *The Garies and Their Friends* (1857), Walter White's *Flight* (1925), John Oliver Killens' *Sippi* (1967), and, more recently, Alice Walker's *Meridian* (1976). These African American authors depict disintegrating interracial relationships for a variety of reasons: to show the need for racial loyalty, the psychological dangers of crossing the color line, and the destructiveness of the racial climate in the United States, and as a bleak reflection of racial tensions in this country. Most novels that portray interracial romance and marriage (whether they are written by white or African American authors) show poisoned, antagonistic, and sensational battlegrounds of racial incompatibility. Andrew's peaceful and harmonious relationship with Peggy demonstrates the power of love to transcend racial categories. As Andrew says, "love conquered the illusion of race, this life-long hallucination that *Thou* and *That* differed" (*OT,* 170), echoing a sentiment that is expressed earlier in the novel, comically, by Karl Marx, who, in this context, is pictured as a householder who preaches the benefits of love. Johnson's radical tutor is disappointed in Marx's solid domesticity. Marx is "a *citizen* devoted first and foremost, to his family" (*OT,* 84). In a familiar and telling act of comic reversal and juxtaposition, Johnson rewrites Marx to downplay Marx's socialist commitment and instead emphasize his personal and spiritual philosophies. With one comic reversal Johnson undercuts the Marxist ideologies that undergird much black cultural nationalist thought.[21]

Although certainly Andrew has been released from the physical and psychological limitations that characterized his enslavement, both allegorical and real, his final position is less an articulation of complete spiritual liberation represented in *moksha* than an enhanced appreciation for his obligations to society as a citizen and as a father. *Moksha,* a Hindu term, is defined as "the end of this cycle [of rebirth] and represents a person's ultimate spiritual goal in Hinduism. The term itself means 'release' and involves primarily a release from karma [cause and effect] and samsara [rebirth, earthly life]. It involves release from all embodied limitations, such as ignorance and suffering. Moksha is the end of births and usually

---

21. For a more complete discussion of this topic, see Jonathan Little, "Charles Johnson's Revolutionary *Oxherding Tale.*"

is characterized as an anonymous, impersonal, blissful state." Andrew has not yet attained this "anonymous, impersonal, blissful state," similar to Kaku-an's oxherder's final position. He is, as spiritual apprentice and householder, beginning on the right path toward ultimate moksha, but he is still in the early stages.[22]

Obstacles

No quest narrative or bildungsroman, however, would be complete without obstacles and complications. Andrew feels a pain in his chest when the Soulcatcher sends him Reb's ring, an Allmuseri ornament, signalling, perhaps, that the Soulcatcher, Bannon, has killed Reb. Searching for Horace, Andrew stumbles upon an illicit slave auction, and his heart problem recurs. As an escaped slave, Andrew has an understandably extreme reaction to the slave auction. First sold are a husband and wife, split up in the auction, instigating another incident in the cycle of families destroyed by slavery. What finally leads Andrew to despair, however, is seeing Minty on the slaveblock; it is the traumatic moment when "the final knot of the heart . . . is broken" (*OT*, 151).

He becomes Master William Harris, as foreshadowed on Reb's puzzling figurine, when he buys Minty for two hundred dollars. Suffering from pellagra, the same disease that killed Reb's wife and daughter, Minty is covered with fever blisters. Andrew has avoided this illness of despair, unlike his father, Patrick, and perhaps Reb, by having, so far, "milked the Self's polymorphy to elude" (*OT*, 155). However, if Minty dies, Andrew predicts that his survival strategy of maintaining a polymorphic and open self will backfire, since he realizes that if he lives through others and they die, he will eventually be destroyed. This is one of the potential dangers, after all, of the spiritually inclusive, integrative being.

When Peggy discovers, through Minty's history, the fictionality of her husband's identity, Johnson rewrites and parodies the sensational and melodramatic African American authored precedents of the interracial couple. Instead of a mawkish sentimental scene in which the outraged wife rejects her husband "stained" by his part-African heritage, Johnson depicts Peggy's reactions differently, thoroughly in concordance with her dedication and love for her husband, despite his racial background. Peggy's reaction, however, cannot save Andrew from the soul-killing despair he suffers when Minty dies of pellegra, which causes the body to disintegrate in a surreal fashion.

22. Kinsley, *Hinduism*, 91.

Freedom

In the final chapter of the novel, Andrew and the Soulcatcher ride into the dark woods, apparently to perform the inevitable destructive act of Andrew's destiny as a runaway bondsman who has lost hope. Through the Soulcatcher's fingers, Andrew feels his heartbeat, which beats "with the pulsethrob of countless bondsmen in his bloodstream, women and children murdered with pistols knives tramped by his warhorse strangled whipped suffocated lynched beheaded burned" (*OT,* 169). In the Soulcatcher's heart, then, is the repository of slavery's horrors in North America—what Toni Morrison calculates as sixty million and more killed through slavery. In his lips Andrew sees a vision of the Middle Passage; the Soulcatcher's body is a pictorial emblem, a cumulative filmic documentary. For Andrew, who now confronts this past and sees his passing for white as a betrayal of his father and all those who are and have been enslaved, the Soulcatcher offers the promise of a quick demise.

Faced with impending death, Andrew realizes that he had never truly escaped slavery. Andrew here defines slavery as "a way of seeing, my inheritance from George Hawkins: *seeing distinctions*" (*OT,* 172). Andrew realizes he is now free of the "egoistic interests that normally colored my vision" (*OT,* 172). Despite this greater philosophical self-awareness, Andrew desires the kill and submits to the Soulcatcher's influence: despair and paranoia, which are the "Negro's private flask of hemlock" (*OT,* 169). The empty fourth panel on Reb's sculpture seems now to have foreshadowed the existential nothingness and absence of Andrew's unhappy and self-destructive death. Yet, it is Reb's strenuous ascetic self-denial that provides Andrew with his own brand of moksha, or release, and saves Andrew from repeating the patterns of self-destruction and loss of hope that characterize many of the other characters in the novel, including his father.

Unexpectedly, the Soulcatcher confesses that Reb eluded him. Since he had made the promise to himself that he would give up if he failed in one of his soul-catching missions, he returns to his wife after he is defeated. In allegorical terms, Negro despair and paranoia have been defeated by the strenuous Zen epistemology of selflessness. On another level, the black cultural nationalist ideology, embodied in George, has fallen before Johnson's phenomenological and spiritual idealism. Unlike George Hawkins, who was an easy kill, Reb is impossible to catch, because "he's *already* free" (*OT,* 173). Since Reb had no appetites, no desires, and no image of himself, the Soulcatcher's aesthetic laws were of no help: "There wasn't no way Ah could git a handhold on the niggah, he was like smoke" (*OT*, 173). "Dead to hope," Reb has no sense of self—he has eradicated the limitations and constrictions of the individual ego and created his own metaphysical and spiritual freedom even within his harsh and soul-killing condition of bondage and servitude. As the Soulcatcher says, he "didn't have no place inside him fo' me to settle. He wasn't *positioned* nowhere" (*OT*, 174). A "Never-Returner" or *Bodhisattva*, Reb has broken out of the repetitive, iterated cycles of birth and death, or the restrictions of *karma* (fate; the law of cause and effect) and *samsara* (the cycle of birth and death) and has moved to a higher level of spiritual achievement. He spiritually and metaphysically anticipates freedom and makes possible his physical freedom. Johnson's rendition of the slave narrative explores the powerful intersection of different kinds of liberation and release from bondage.

The Final Epiphany

In the final chapter of the novel, Andrew is granted his own glimpse of mystical holism. In a surreal vision that is projected on the chest of the Soulcatcher, Andrew sees the essential rhythms of the universe, the inevitable cycles of creation and destruction. In this "impossible flesh tapestry of a thousand individualities no longer static, mere drawings, but if you looked at them long enough, bodies moving like Lilliputians over the surface of his skin. Not tattoos at all" (*OT*, 175). Through this vision Andrew witnesses Bannon's murderous history as a slave catcher and bounty hunter and watches that history merge with his own and with the cycle of life and death of the universe, in which "the commonwealth of the dead shape-shifted on his chest," (*OT* 175). In this hallucinatory, transcendental vision the static, cartoonish tattoos begin moving to form a fluid and metamorphizing narrative. Johnson captures the transition from the static caricature of cartooning to the fluid complexities offered by literary prose, thereby inscribing the history of his own artistic or aesthetic metamorphosis onto Andrew's sea change of consciousness, in which he moves from a primarily ego-centered Western perspective to a Buddhist and Hindu conception of the benefits of the loss of self. Aesthetic technique and medium merge with perceptual transition.

In his vividly rendered epiphany, Andrew experiences "the profound mystery of the One and the Many," and is liberated from his individualistic psychological and spiritual bondage. Now his father's love has been given back, "in every being from grubworms to giant sumacs" (*OT*, 176), to him again and again—thus healing the destructive estrangement that had arisen between father and son, especially after Andrew decided to pass for white and marry a white woman to escape from slavery, decisions his father forbade. In his rendition of Eastern spiritualism and the related romantic worship of nature, Johnson argues that nothing has been lost in Andrew's painful passage to liberation; instead, he has absorbed everything within him and has profoundly benefited from this integrative universal absorption. This mystical passage emphasizes the union of father and son and the indwelling spirit of his father's love throughout nature and the expansive, non-linear cycle of the universe and history.

The Bannon moving-tattoo scene bears a striking resemblance to the climax of Hesse's *Siddhartha*. At the end of that novel there is a similar efflorescence or explosion of meaning. In Hesse's novel, Govinda, Siddhartha's childhood friend, experiences the fluid interconnectedness of all forms of life in a continuous and filmic vision as Siddhartha kisses his forehead. All the faces he sees "all came and disappeared and yet all seemed to be there at the same time, which all continually changed and renewed themselves and which were yet all Siddhartha . . . He saw all these forms and faces in a thousand relationships to each other, all helping each other, loving, hating and destroying each other and become newly born." In this passage by Hesse inspired by Eastern philosophy, the universe rhythmically represents itself through different forms in a similar cycle of interconnected birth, death, and rebirth. While *Oxherding Tale* is more than just a rearticulation of *Siddhartha* within a different historical and racial context, it owes much to Hesse's novel in terms of the structure and style of its ultimate epiphany. Through *Siddhartha*'s intertextual presence, Johnson performs a complex act of literary echoing. Just as the Westerner Hesse interpreted and imagined the life of the Buddha, Johnson draws from original Zen, Buddhist, and Hindu beliefs and sources, merging them with European interpretations, such as Hesse's and his own distinctive imaginative variations. In so doing, Johnson demonstrates the expansive range of his literary echoing, unconfined by American or African American precedents.[23]

While *Oxherding Tale* also replicates aspects of Kaku-an's *Ten Oxherding Pictures*, the final passage in Johnson's novel demonstrates *Oxherding Tale*'s difference. Instead of living in a state of enigmatic passivity and detachment, Andrew abides in a state of self-redefinition that is still dependent on the proliferation of his ego-forms (he sees himself in the filmic panorama on the Soulcatcher's chest) and, to some extent, on the existence of his wife. Together they build a new, mutual identity. While now deeply aware of the unity and fluidity of all forms, Andrew has not achieved the

---

23. Hesse, *Siddhartha*, 150.

state of blissful nirvana or self-detachment that is achieved in Kaku-an's self-nihilating narrative. Unlike the oxherder, Andrew does not become a magic, larger-than-life, spiritually charged force capable of touching dead trees into life. The final chapter is deceptively entitled *"Moksha"* since Andrew does not, as an apprentice Hindu householder, attain the kind of final enlightenment or spiritual release that *moksha* implies. Andrew's personalized *moksha* may be his liberation from physical and metaphysical bondage, and recognition that he is on the Buddhist path now to attaining his final spiritual goal, but he has certainly not yet attained that final, otherworldly state.

Further placing Johnson's *Oxherding Tale* within the frame of Hinduism, the Soulcatcher is appropriately referred to as Shiva's hitman. Like Shiva, the Soulcatcher controls the process of creation and destruction. In Hindu mythology, Shiva is a central god who dances out the dance of the universe; he "conveys an orderly, refined, rhythmic grace that suggests universal order and refinement . . . Shiva's dance is the orderly dance of life, nature, and the physical cosmos generally." Included in this cosmic dance is a period of total destruction in which "the world is burned to ashes." Indulging his appetite for murder and destruction, the Soulcatcher aptly emulates Shiva's playful detachment from human suffering.[24]

Andrew's hallucinatory perception that George Hawkins has been absorbed into nature repeats the epiphany in *Faith and the Good Thing* where Faith's father, Todd Cross, became interfused with nature. For both central characters, these fundamentally romantic epiphanies are consoling—they provide enough psychological and spiritual release to allow them to break out of the self-destructive cycle they inherited, while incorporating the suffering and totality of their histories that have preceded them in their evolving identities. Where Faith becomes a "life-artist," so too, in a different way, does Andrew. With his wife Peggy, Andrew "turns to the process of rebuilding . . . the world" (*OT*, 176) through their daughter, Anna, who replaces/doubles Andrew's dead mother, Anna Polkinghorne. Just as Reb, the quintessential Zen Buddhist rebel and life-artist, creates his masterpiece, the coffin for Abraham Lincoln, Andrew conjures his retrospective tale as the provisional narrator and "rebuilds" the world through his children and his tale. In Reb's characterization, Johnson hints tantalizingly at a movement toward instead of away from the world. Thus Johnson modifies the narrative arc taken by the oxherder in *Ten Oxherding Pictures,* who remains removed from and incomprehensible to common humanity at the end of his narrative.

24. Kinsley, *Hinduism,* 180.

This final epiphany, in which Andrew reconciles with his father, is significant in terms of Johnson's aesthetic. Firstly, it echoes the spiritual impulse that informs the sacred trickster figure from *Faith and the Good Thing*. Secondly, it dramatizes Johnson's self-professed ideology-free or politically neutral aesthetic. It indicates Johnson's rejection of explicitly politically motivated protest fiction since, in this holistic vision nature's metamorphosis has "no purpose beyond the delight the universe took in diversity for its own sake, the proliferation of beauty . . ." (*OT*, 175). The universe becomes the ultimate artistic force, creating beauty and multiple forms for no purpose other than the proliferation of beauty, which echoes Walter Pater's famous dictum, art for art's sake. Except for Johnson, art has become indistinguishable from the rhythms of a spiritually charged nature.

Similarly, in *Being and Race* Johnson writes that he looks forward to the time when African American literature and culture can "move from narrow complaint to broad celebration" (*BR*, 123), tied to no particular ideology. For Johnson, the connections between criticism, the slave narrative, and aesthetics are deep indeed. As he writes, "The idea suits me down to the ground, the possibility that our art can be dangerous and wickedly diverse, enslaved to no single idea of Being, capable of unraveling, like Penelope, all that was spun the night before" (*BR*, 122). Unanswered in these art-for-art's sake arguments is the extent to which even this wish to avoid ideology is informed by an integrationist ideology, which inclusively seeks out diverse perspectives à la Faith's final synthetic position. Certainly *Oxherding Tale* can be read as a subtle argument for reversing the movement toward Black Power segregationist thinking back toward an integrationist ideal. At the same time the novel is more than a political or ideological statement in its complex merger of aesthetics, spirituality, politics, history, and diverse literary precedents.

Thirdly, Andrew's final epiphany demonstrates a subtle shift in Johnson's previously solipsistic vision. In *Faith and the Good Thing*, Johnson seemed content to end with a position that inhabited a relatively isolated place—the realm of aesthetics, philosophy, and art. Faith ended as a brilliant life artist, adopting different roles and interested in pursuing new paths and new knowledge mostly for her own benefit and self-development, while at the same time representing a deeply communal symbol, the trickster. At the end of *Oxherding Tale,* however, Johnson is moving toward a more socially oriented aesthetic, one that expands his previously individualistic conclusions. He does not end with Andrew becoming the magical and removed oxherder; he is instead a dedicated member of the social community, a Hindu-inspired householder. And, within the moving flesh tapestry, Andrew sees a commonwealth of shapes and forms that represent the chaotic amalgamation of all human societies. In the body mosaic Andrew envisions, there is "a society as complex as the higher forms" (*OT*, 175) to which Andrew feels an intimate connection. While the emphasis is certainly on the main character's philosophical and spiritual movement toward liberation and newfound freedom, metaphysical and physical (a characteristic of the slave narrative genre), the novel signals Johnson's first movement outward to connect the individual with the society at large.

This evolved position ultimately undercuts Ashraf Rushdy's argument that *Oxherding Tale* is primarily a postmodern text. While Rushdy is right to emphasize Johnson's phenomenological and postmodern rebellion against "the spurious concept not only of 'race,' but also of 'personal identity,'" to read *Oxherding Tale* and Johnson's phenomenological orientation and achievement as "a symbol for the postmodern condition" underemphasizes Johnson's profoundly liberal humanist thrust. In Andrew's final vision he merges with the "profound mystery of the One and the Many" (*OT*, 175). Andrew realizes the interconnectedness, mutuality, and interdependence of all forms when he envisions this complex commonwealth or society on the Soulcatcher's chest. This integrative vision would seem to work against postmodernism's emphasis on fragmentation, privatization, and rejection of both globalized unity and individual transcendence through religion.[25]

Johnson's novel is curiously traditional as well. Johnson engages non-African American intertextual sources to further the rhetorical appeal of quintessential slave narratives such as Frederick Douglass's *Narrative of the Life of Frederick Douglass* and novelistic treatments of slavery such as William Wells Brown's *Clotelle; or, The Colored Heroine* to protest slavery's inhumanity. Both the nineteenth-century slave narratives and Johnson's neo-slave narrative rendition provide strategies and models of humanity that inspire their readers and offer them new perspectives on African American identity.

Certainly, the charge could be made against Johnson that his reliance on Eastern mysticism and the integrative identity leads to a profound loss of ethnic empowerment and being as the ethnic self vanishes into the mainstream of dominant society. Nowhere in Johnson's works do we see an evocation of the humanely ethnocentric or the possibilities of an inspired nationalism that seeks to maintain a communal identity while

---

25. Ashraf Rushdy, "The Phenomenology of the Allmuseri: Charles Johnson and the Subject of the Narrative of Slavery," 386.

at the same time avoiding lapses into discriminatory racial chauvinism. Johnson's solutions of absorbing other identities and giving up individual identity in the interests of the larger whole, while spiritually and philosophically well thought out and intriguing, contain within them the dangers of invisibility and the disempowerment that is often foisted on members of oppressed minorities and ethnic groups to maintain the economic and cultural status quo. The more problematic aspects of his integrative vision are addressed not so much in his novels as in his short stories, where, for the first time, Johnson comes face to face with its potential shortcomings. For that reason his short stories reveal, in vignette form, some of the most penetrating insights in his literary career. As I explore Johnson's short stories I will explore the thesis that perhaps it is the legacy of the slave narrative's structure, which relies on the ascent from bondage to liberation, that overly controls Johnson's novels, forcing them, in a sense, to embrace, at the end, an integrationist vision. The abbreviated short story form often disallows such an embracing vision.

4

Staring into the Abyss

The Sorcerer's Apprentice

Johnson's only collection of short stories, *The Sorcerer's Apprentice* (1982), presents a strikingly different vision from that of his novels. While his stories explore familiar themes—individual transformations, the benefits of spirituality and intercultural synthesis, the power of art—Johnson's conclusions are surprisingly pessimistic and grim. In these *Tales and Conjurations,* the collection's subtitle, Johnson dwells on the nightmarish and destructive side of his integrative aesthetic and social vision. Johnson varies the form of his stories—the fairy tale, the fable, the parable, the science fiction fantasy—to depict American society teetering on the edge of the abyss, propelled toward disunification by a tragic and irrevocable history of racism. Just as one of Johnson's African American characters fears for his sanity in a white-dominated world, Johnson's short stories generally focus on the pain and suffering of African American existence, unalleviated by the possibility of spiritual transcendence.

Slavery's Legacy

Johnson opens the collection with a searing New Testament parable, "The Education of Mingo," that explores the destructive effects of slavery through a shocking allegory of artistic creation gone awry. Like *Oxherding Tale,* "The Education of Mingo" is set in slaveholding nineteenth-century America. Unlike *Oxherding Tale,* however, the point of view has been altered. In this story Johnson uses a third-person limited-omniscient point of view, focused on the rigid perspective of the slave owner Moses Green.

109

This brief and complex story captures Moses's dawning awareness of the irreparable harm he has wrought through his slaveholding status, father surrogacy, and artistic aspirations. "The Education of Mingo" as a statement of Johnson's anti-aesthetic foreshadows the collection's pervasive mood of self-reflexive doubt.

Johnson's by now familiar dialogue about aesthetics is on the surface of the story. When farmer Moses Green buys a slave named Mingo, he feels "like an artist" (*SA*, 5), shaping a lump of clay. To Moses, Mingo is the exotic other, childlike and vulnerable. As an artist, Moses wants to colonialize, civilize, and christianize Mingo, to remake him in the Anglo-Christian image and to whiten him, at least on the inside.

Moses's aesthetic compulsion is clear and clearly dangerous. Through Mingo, his selfish creation, Moses hopes to domesticate the exotic other and to promote what Moses considers "the good." Johnson portrays Moses as the didactic and polemic artist, unwilling to empty himself first, before artistic creation, as does Reb, or to try different paths of knowledge, as does Faith.

Moses's inflexible aesthetic modus operandi is characterized by the nineteenth-century melting-pot metaphor of assimilation, purifying or obliterating one worldview and replacing it with another. Thus Moses is pleased when, within a year, Mingo adheres to his perspective in terms of his gestures, his actions, and his likes and dislikes. Yet, Moses is anxious about his artistic product and the potential of his loss of control.

Juxtaposed to Moses, the misguided and dangerous artist, is Moses's lady friend, Harriet Bridgewater. She is a romantic conjurer in the tradition of Faith Cross and Evelyn Pomeroy. Her voice reminds Moses of a song: she is able to "sing a sunset more beautiful—like the good Lord coming in a cloud" (*SA*, 8). Because of her intuitive conjuring artistry, Harriet is the voice of wisdom in the story. She warns Moses against playing God and reminds him that slaves are generally unpredictable. In short, she believes Moses is making a mistake in trying to reshape and transform his slave. Moses resists her wisdom and revels in his artistic achievement. To him, Mingo is an appendage made in his own image, who has successfully embodied his initial aesthetic motivations.

Predictably—given Johnson's bias against didactic literature—Moses's rigid aesthetic vision quickly unravels. Mingo enacts Moses's deepest impulses by killing a neighbor. When Moses sees Isaiah's dead body, he experiences feelings of dislocation and alienation not unlike Faith's initial stage of fear and uncertainty. His worldview and presuppositions have been severely challenged and overturned. When Mingo kills Harriet Bridgewater, Moses is introduced to unpredictability and to the problematics of his artistic assimilative approach. Moses himself had fantasized about killing Harriet, and his artistic product has become a frightening shadow; violently enacting that which Moses sought to keep hidden. Although finally denied the same liberation and empowerment as Reb in *Oxherding Tale,* Mingo seizes control of his master by employing Reb's technique of egoless listening, or imaginative variation.

Through Mingo's gradual attainment of power, Moses is brought face to face with his loss of artistic control. Instead of being the creator, Moses now feels that he and Mingo "were wired together" (*SA*, 15). Moses is horrifically and inextricably linked to Mingo and is in the grip of external forces. What started out for Moses as a parable of cultural whitewashing and nineteenth-century melting-pot ideology has become a nightmare of cultural intermixture and the unethical and self-destructive interfusion of American and African, which is a reversal of much of Johnson's previous fiction.

As the story continues, Johnson changes its focus. It becomes Johnson's parable of aesthetics and identity. Moses finally realizes the impossibility of enslaving another human being; he also learns that "It was a bitter thing to siphon your being from someone else" (*SA*, 18). What began as Mingo's education becomes Moses's and then Johnson's.

Moses's education and acquisition of cultural and racial sensitivity comes too late however—he is caught in a fatalistic, Faulknerian dilemma of racial interconnection based on the imbalance of power and a legacy of inhumanity and suffering. One violent act—instigated by Moses's violent aesthetics—leads, in a kind of karmic sequence, inevitably to another, and Mingo kills yet again. Moses accepts his guilt and understands that Mingo will never completely become him, especially given his particularistic background and cultural perspective. Moses learns the truth of Harriet Bridgewater's warnings against playing God and yielding to artistic vanity.

In however perverted a form, Mingo is still Moses's world recreated and sustained. They are thus tragically intertwined, white and black together in a deadly dance of forced kinship and artistic pride. As they plan their escape and begin their ride west toward Missouri, they seem physically connected, "like fugitives with no fingers" (*SA*, 19), as Moses thinks. The artistic touch Moses used to turn a lump of clay into his Frankenstein creation, Mingo, is gone; Moses is fingerless, unable to change, refashion, or in any way alter his actions or artistic decisions of the past. The two men are joined together, white and black, in a rigid parable preaching against the sins of aesthetic pride. Moses's initial desire to use Mingo, his artistic product, as a didactic device to cultivate good and cripple evil now seems ironic. Tragically, Mingo has become the evil and flawed Moses that Moses was trying to repress.

"The Education of Mingo" operates on several allegorical levels at once. The New Testament parable identifies the sins of vanity and pride. The social and historical allegory identifies the tragic results of slavery for blacks and whites in the North American context and also casts doubt on Johnson's pervasively integrationist social vision, which involves the interpenetration of different cultures and identities and the belief in universals and cross-cultural commonalities. This short story suggests an anti-integrative ideology, one that does not involve the absorption of one cultural, historical, and racial identity into another. It implies that what should be promoted is the reverse—the perpetuation of a singular mainstream culture and the maintenance and preservation of separate cultures for the healthy survival of all who participate in the frightening dance of racial relatedness. Such a story, freighted with ideological implications, seems to contradict or at least problematize Johnson's emergent integrationist thinking.

At its deepest level of reflexivity, perhaps this story is also a meditation on the limitations of Johnson's aesthetic. Perhaps *he,* through his didactic intent, becomes linked, inextricably, to his characters and loses control, becomes fingerless, and, in the grip of larger, unseen, and deterministic forces, lets his moralistic impulses gain control. Johnson, in working through the parable form, becomes controlled by didacticism. Like Moses, Johnson uses the parable (or is used by the parable) to blast away at evil and to promote the good in a way that recalls Gardner's rather simplistic formula for serious fiction and subverts the more freewheeling ambiguity of Faith's final position as a goddess of phenomenological artistic freedom. As such "The Education of Mingo" is, like the other stories in the collection, a frightening reflection of Johnson's other works—acting out in nightmarish reverse the themes and figures that were promoted and developed in his novels, especially in their denouements.

Exchange Value

While "The Education of Mingo," first published in 1977, can be seen as the distorted shadow of *Faith and the Good Thing,* the next story in the collection, "Exchange Value," originally published in 1982, can be seen as a bitterly ironic commentary on *Oxherding Tale,* also published in 1982. Unlike the benign cosmic spiritual harmony achieved in the end of *Oxherding Tale,* "Exchange Value" limns the harsh realistic truth that African Americans are often psychologically destroyed by their socioeconomic conditions.

Two brothers living in the projects on Chicago's infamous south side stumble across a incredible fortune, an inheritance that should physically and perhaps metaphysically liberate them, especially in the context of attaining the materialistic American dream. The two brothers, Loftis and Cooter, the narrator, target a West Indian neighbor, Miss Bailey, for robbery. When they notice that her mail is not being collected, they think she has gone out of town. They break into her apartment, and what they find taxes their imaginations—it is a veritable repository of American wealth and luxury. Johnson blurs the boundaries between realism and fantasy in having his two characters enter a symbolic setting that encapsulates America's history and capitalistic materialism. Inside is a dazzling array of collected items, including World War II magazines, silver dollars, rings, safes, and a Model A Ford. This clearly mythic scene is North American history in reverse as its description progresses back, in retrograde order, past the fuel-burning stove, past World War II, past the Model A Ford to a chopped-up tree, all the while saturated with images of money. This symbolic landscape identifies all the things that Loftis, Cooter, Miss Bailey and their parents and their parents' parents and so on have been denied because of the color of their skin.

Miss Bailey's wealth is like sorcery; it is magical, unfulfilled promise. Cooter wants to release the genie of materialism and use Miss Bailey's property to transform it magically into other things. They have stumbled into Aladdin's cave of wonders from *Arabian Nights,* and yet they, like Miss Bailey, who hoarded the treasure all her life and lived in poverty, are paralyzed, unable to release the magic of the money, unable to take advantage of its powerful potential because of the psychological damage they have suffered.

The brothers become cursed by the money. Instead of liberating them, its conjured spell further traps and restricts them. Loftis now simply takes the place of Miss Bailey as hoarder and miser. After they move her inheritance into their apartment, he forbids his brother to spend a penny of the money, because, he explains, "As soon as you buy something you *lose* the power to buy something" (*SA*, 36). He suffers, as did Miss Bailey, from "that special Negro fear of using up what little we get in this life" (*SA*, 37). Both Miss Bailey and Loftis are spellbound by the money and obsessed by their fear of squandering this denied power. Creeping into Loftis's room while he is asleep, the narrator realizes that his brother is paralyzed by his situation. Cooter's hope that he and Loftis can avoid the miserly and miserable fate of Miss Bailey is undermined by his final symbolic action of placing a penny into Miss Bailey's jar and carefully storing the jar with the rest of the items.

Through "Exchange Value," Johnson dramatizes the devastating effects of years of discrimination and economic deprivation on African Americans. Cooter and Loftis are prohibited from invoking the spell of money, of letting its magic work for them by their shared neuroses. Cooter is not allowed, despite his wishes, to immerse himself in "a world inside the world," into the "picturebook scenes of plentifulness" (*SA*, 30). Instead of living in an idealized artistically rendered state of being—the picturebook—the brother's state resembles more the harsh legacy of realism and naturalism passed on by Richard Wright's powerful vision of terror. Miss Bailey, for example, still lies in the apartment, a maggot-eaten corpse. Loftis, despite his self-reflexivity, seems headed for the same fate, another casualty of that special African American fear. The anger of Bigger Thomas, who wanted the affluence enjoyed by the white people of Chicago's Hyde Park, seems to have been internalized and repeated in this story—the violence moving inward toward self-destruction. The rat that figures so prominently in the unforgettable opening scene of Wright's *Native Son* is figuratively and horrifically gnawing away at these characters' insides, and when Cooter and Loftis find Miss Bailey's body, they discover a rat is literally inside her.

Johnson denies his characters the same release of self-affirming violence that Wright offers Bigger in *Native Son*. In these opening stories he also denies his characters the liberating resolutions through art, African spiritualism, and phenomenology that he allows Faith in *Faith and the Good Thing*. Certainly the focus of these stories is far away from the integrative spirituality that informs *Oxherding Tale*. Instead, taken as a pair, "The Education of Mingo" and "Exchange Value" deny the magic of art, by showing how conjuration can quickly become a curse or a spell that cannot be broken and by showing the problems of assimilation. As Cooter says when he first sees Miss Bailey's inheritance, "And I be sure the lady's stuff had a terrible string attached" (*SA*, 32); that terrible string is the tragic past of North American race relations—that deadly, overwhelming legacy.

Social Catastrophe

Johnson's expression of anger and despair continues in "Menagerie: A Child's Fable." The wide-scale social disintegration and racial warfare envisioned in this story seems the logical next step given the injustices and oppression depicted in the first two stories. Yet, the catastrophic balkanization and social disintegration that occurs in "Menagerie" is due less to any history of oppression or racism than to the flawed philosophical and political positions of essentialism and identity politics that have been voiced in contemporary debates about multiculturalism. At the same time, "Menagerie," through negative implication, suggests possibilities for social and racial healing.

This fable is a thinly veiled social and philosophical commentary. When Berkeley, the watchdog of a pet shop, discovers that his owner, Mr. Tilford, has mysteriously disappeared, leaving him in charge, he quickly discovers the chaos and difficulties of North American pluralism. The pet shop is a chaotic mixture of individual and group demands that threatens the unity and survival of the abandoned shop. The philosophical and political claims of a "distinct and inviolable nature" (*SA*, 46) (i.e., essentialism) leads only to complete confusion. The narrator's tone suggests the irony in the essentialists' position, implying that they only think they have inviolable, essential natures, when, in fact, they do not. This irony anticipates the spiritual revelation later in the story, which dramatizes a longing for universality and brotherhood across the chasms of race, nationalities, and gender. The story shows the inevitable escalation of conflict between differing viewpoints and perspectives, especially when they are tied to essentialist claims. The story is a direct commentary and warning against the dangers brought on by flawed philosophical perspectives based on dualistic thinking, especially on particularism, factionalism, and identity politics.

Berkeley's antagonist is Monkey, who, analyzing the situation carefully, devises a rhetorical strategy to convince Berkeley to release the caged animals. A group of insurgents, led by Monkey, makes increasingly vehement claims of self-determination and group power that escalate into charges that their leader, Berkeley, is a fascist. Berkeley seems helpless against this charge and, seeing no other way to placate the insurgents, follows Monkey's advice, despite its obvious dangers. Berkeley is able to maintain order only because he is the biggest; yet he is uncomfortable with his leadership role since he had flattered himself into thinking that he was given this role as a result of his intelligence. Through Berkeley's ironic self-realization, Johnson conveys the irony of his own belief that phenomenological imaginative variation can affect positive social change. Instead, what matters, sadly, is deadly, violent force.

The death of God is symbolized by the departure of Tilford, the pet shop's owner. Berkeley is horrified by the thought that Tilford might be dead or unconcerned with their crises. Thus, in the absence of a greater being, the characters are forced to look to themselves for solutions and systems of harmonious government and society. But Berkeley's power quickly fails: "Cracks, then fissures began to appear, it seemed to Berkeley, everywhere" (*SA*, 53). Each species has its own demands for special treatment. The polarization and conflict spreads from racial claims of superiority to deep-seated antagonism between the sexes.

To escape from this chaos and disorder, Berkeley falls asleep and nostalgically dreams of Tilford's return. The dream builds to a mystical vision of unity and connection, the "colorless light behind the owner so blinding it obliterated their outlines, blurred their precious differences" (*SA*, 56). This overpowering vision of underlying universals and commonalities silences the conflicts that have erupted and replaces internecine warfare with cooperation and harmony. In articulating the preposterousness and outrageousness of overly politicized individual identity, Johnson spiritualizes a previously secularized pluralistic democracy. In an application of Buddhist and Christian divine immanence, the narrator attacks the notions of distinctiveness and the illusion of a separate self standing apart from the communal good. Buddhism's chief emphasis is on the eradication of suffering through the elimination of ego, of the belief in individual identity. And, in a "burst of preternatural brilliance that rayed the whole room" (*SA*, 56), Berkeley dreams of Tilford's approval. Johnson fuses the Christian and the Buddhist tradition into one—emphasizing the combined synthetic power of spirituality to eradicate and cure human difference and conflict.

Yet the dream of unification and harmony—King's "beloved community"—is only an artistically shaped illusion, since Berkeley's dreamy alternative is replaced by the destructiveness and reality of aggressive identity politics. He wakes to an attack. With blood coursing out of his body, Berkeley lives only long enough to see the carnage and destruction that took place while he slept. Various groups of warring animals tore each other apart. Johnson alternately gestures toward possible solutions and erases them. The mythopoetic solutions we have come to anticipate are encased in this story in a fragile dream that is quickly destroyed by exposure to the reality of contemporary political ideologies.

The story also suggests that the catastrophe and destruction that result are in part due to a lack of shared spiritual vision and belief. The echoing void of Tortoise's shell as he smirks at the destruction suggests a nihilistic and secular alternative to the light that had filled the room in Berkeley's wishful dream of salvation and divinity. That Johnson ended on such a grim note emphasizes his predominately religious impulse.

This fable is an apocalyptic commentary on the contemporary culture wars, a virtual jeremiad against the supporters of ethnic and gender particularization and essentialism. In the highly charged contemporary context of the culture wars, however, this story is not an apology for Western Christian values. Through its synthetic merger of Christian, Buddhist, and

Hindu philosophies and theologies, the story shows the decisive power of intercultural, interfaith mixture as a compelling antidote to divisive postmodern society's woes. Thus a story that at first glance may look like an implicit argument against multiculturalism and diversity and for the hegemony of a single cultural and racial power, becomes, on review, a subtle argument *for* globalized unity and the powers of universals. Instead of being an apology for Eurocentric uniformity and control, it is a plea for integration beyond the level of racial, national, and sexual differences. In this way "Menagerie: A Child's Fable," departs from the first two stories in the collection; it merely repeats, although in somewhat heavy-handed fashion, the ideological conclusions of much of Johnson's other work. First published in 1984, it is a pivotal story for Johnson since it demonstrates a continued move, begun by *Oxherding Tale*, toward the social application of his thinking, a move he will complete when writing *Middle Passage* in addressing the state of the democratic republic.

Oxherding Tale Revisited

While the first three stories of the collection have clearly stressed the disintegration of self and society, "China" offers a possible solution, at least for individuals seeking to revitalize and heal their own illnesses, reminiscent of the denouement of *Oxherding Tale*, which was published one year earlier than the short story. "China" is an experiment in the Carveresque form of realistic minimalism. Instead of working within the realm of the antirealistic, and the fantastic, as in "Menagerie: A Child's Fable," "China" returns to the mundane in its depiction of an aging couple's day-to-day life.

The main characters, Rudolph and Evelyn, both in their early fifties, have been disappointed in life and have surrendered to a kind of living death; they are the "dead living," the condition that Faith manages to escape through her immersion into folkloric myth and magic. For this couple, however, marriage is a slow suicide pact. Johnson varies from his usual male-oriented point of view by telling it from a women's perspective in limited omniscient. Her only comfort is the knowledge that Rudolph is in poorer health than she. In an interesting inversion concerning the power of Christianity, Evelyn sees an affirmation of the eventual loss of energy and death in the Jesus statue that adorns their home. She seems resigned to her growing blindness, which is symbolic of her gradual loss of life-sustaining aesthetic vision.

Just as in *Faith and the Good Thing*, where Faith escapes her condition of marital death-in-life when she becomes a premier life-artist and conjurer and accepts an alternate form of magical African spirituality, the characters in "China" rebel against the conditions in African American life through an empowering and enlightening infusion of Eastern culture. The magic appears to be this ability to learn from and assimilate other cultures. Johnson depicts Rudolph's sudden and passionate dedication to learning kung fu, which leads him to Zen Buddhist meditation and an increased sense of community.

In *Being and Race,* the chapter "Being and Form" is devoted to a discussion of the martial arts and to writing, since "it's fair to compare the severe discipline of the Asian martial arts to writing" (*BR*, 47). According to Johnson, it is important for the apprentice writer to first master the forms he or she inherits, such as the sketch, fable, yarn, and tale as a way to connect with the "brilliance of our predecessors and their inevitable oversights and omissions—the limits of their understanding" (*BR*, 48). Similarly, in the martial arts, students are expected to honor and recombine the inherited forms to the best of their abilities. In writing and art more than in the strict discipline of the martial arts it would seem that "Cross-cultural fertilization keeps the form alive. Saves it from senility. And death" (*BR*, 47). Through his disciplined practice, Rudolph saves himself from senility and death. His health improves, and he becomes a fit physical specimen, correcting his earlier high blood pressure and heart problems. By honoring the forms of Asian martial arts, Rudolph demonstrates allegorically the rewards of formalist and imaginative variation, technical virtuosity and cross-cultural fertilization in literature. He has expanded his self or form beyond its previous confines and has thus attained a certain strength and vitality. As a fulfillment of Johnson's integrationist aesthetic, Rudolph has become a more complex, healthier, cross-cultural "form." To highlight Rudolph's symbolic role as aesthetic vehicle, Evelyn reports that he refines his form by practicing in front of the mirror.

Rudolph's personal advancement as a collective being carries with it certain tangible social rewards. Through his kung fu class, or kwoon, Rudolph joins a integrative spiritual community and experiences fellowship that he previously lacked. The differences between the martial arts students are blurred by their passionate involvement in their craft, and their presence threatens Evelyn. The kwoon comprises students from the University of Washington, including a Vietnamese immigrant and a Puerto Rican. Through their shared devotion to an ancient craft, these artists overcome the boundaries of race, class, and gender.

This same integrative message is repeated in a more recent story, "Kwoon," published in 1991. The kwoon is a South Side Chicago martial arts studio, and the story concerns the efforts of the studio's owner to keep the business open. David Lewis's legitimacy as a teacher is challenged by a forty-year-old man, Ed Morgan, who is the exemplar of Johnson's ideals about art and cross-fertilization. Morgan's eclectic mastery of kung fu is dazzling: "The older man shifted from boxing to *wu*-style *ta' chi Chuan*. From this he flowed into *pa kua,* then Korean karate: style after style, a blending of a dozen cultures and histories in one blink of an eye after another." Morgan, at first resentful and skeptical of Lewis's leadership, gradually gains a deep respect for the kwoon and for the school Lewis has created. At the end of the story he discovers in Lewis a masterful teacher—despite the fact that he had beaten him—one who has created the supportive, spiritually unified community for which he has been searching his whole transient life. In the gradual assimilation of Morgan into the kwoon, the story upholds Lewis's "hidden agenda" in running the studio in such an economically deprived area, which is to encourage "an inward training that would make the need for conflict fall away like chrysalis." Unlike "China," "Kwoon" erases race as a factor, yet it, like "China," emphasizes the empowering communal aspect of the martial arts, which is merely a dramatization or enactment of the Buddhist principles of reverence for the past, a commitment to the community, selflessness, and strenuous self-discipline.[1]

In "China," Rudolph too becomes a vehicle for Johnson's Buddhist values and program for eliminating conflict. Through Rudolph, Johnson counters the mood of victimization, alienation, and isolation that informs "Exchange Value" and, later in the collection, "Popper's Disease." In this collection, "China" engages the previous more pessimistic stories in an internal dialogue that illuminates the complex nuances, rhythms, and opposition of his own perceptions of the possibilities and restrictions of African American life.

There is a more subtle correlation between Rudolph's developing mysticism and the aesthetics rendered through "China's" symbolism. At the beginning of the story, Evelyn feels her own encroaching blindness. Rudolph's vision is enhanced, even cured, through his meditative and strenuous journey into the self, where he becomes one with the canvas and the members of his kwoon; Evelyn takes longer to regain and achieve full vision. Thus the story contains two accounts of individual liberation, one following and dependent upon the other.

During his meditations, Rudolph's insights are described using visual imagery and analogies. During zazen, Zen "just sitting" meditation, Rudolph withdraws into himself, picturing himself at the bottom of Lake

---

1. Charles Johnson, "Kwoon," 328, 326.

Washington. There he disciplines his mind to achieve one point of concentration until "he slipped deeper into the vortices of himself, into the Void—even the image of himself on the lake floor vanished" (*SA*, 87). Through this Zen meditative process of making himself the focal point, he paradoxically breaks free from himself and from his illusion of individual identity. Thus, he merges with his mental canvas and temporarily resolves the subject-object dualistic split that, according to Zen (and to Johnson), leads to sickness, suffering, and decay.

Rudolph is at once empowered and revitalized through his rigorous training and meditation. His improvements of self, however, do not lead to the kind of social salvation that is suggested in Berkeley's dream of Tilford's return. Instead, his insights draw him farther into himself. The story's focus remains trained on Evelyn's expanding personal perception. Her transformation comes when watching Rudolph perform in Seattle's Kingdome in a kung fu tournament. At first she miserably reflects that, given her husband's change, he will now outlive her and move on to marry another, younger woman after her death. Then she achieves a moment of small liberation when she can suddenly see better in a newly appreciated vision of her husband flying through the air during the tournament: "at that moment, the fighting in the farthest ring, in herself, perhaps in all the world, was over" (*SA*, 95). Evelyn's final revelation echoes and exemplifies the story's epigraph, which is drawn from *The Dhammapada*, the sayings of the Buddha, transcribed the first century before Christ. "If one man conquer in battle a thousand men, and if another conquers himself, he is the greatest of all conquerors." This passage comes from the chapter "The Thousands," which begins, "Better than a thousand hollow words / Is one word that brings peace." Johnson is drawing from the Buddhist assumption that this meditative self-improvement will have effects on the larger social whole. Words can indeed bring peace. Thus there are two rings in which the fighting is resolved in the closing sentence: the ring within Evelyn and "perhaps" in the entire world. Yet, because Johnson modifies the fighting in all the world with "perhaps," it is clear that he is leaving that social connection unproven and merely suggested.[2]

Instead of stressing her transformation's social significance—its ability to produce peace, for instance—Johnson is content to emphasize the aesthetic and the individual, even in his depiction of the spiritual community, or kwoon, which remains, despite its closeness, an exclusive and self-contained group of dedicated kung fu practitioners. This same

---

2. Thomas Byrom, *Dhammapada*, 30.

inner-directedness is true as well in "Kwoon," in which Lewis realized early in his martial arts training that "in his spirit he had resources greater than anything in the world outside." Johnson will take the final steps in translating his belief in spiritual community to the larger canvas of national identity, specifically in *Middle Passage* and in the utopian post-apocalyptic short story "The Work of the World."[3]

Instead of a larger social vision, the private picture Evelyn focuses on is a single vision of her husband, as if it were one frame of a film. Thus she fictionalizes or dramatizes his life—his Zen Buddhist aspirations have restored her sight of him as a character in a film, since in the beginning of the story, her failing sight is analogized as "the sudden shock of an empty frame in a series of slides" (*SA*, 64). Evelyn moves into the position of the creative artist at the end of the story, replacing her athletic husband as the story's central character. Johnson draws a clear line from the empowering aesthetic technique—in this case symbolized through kung fu—to aesthetic liberation. By vicariously participating in her husband's newfound artistic power, Evelyn heals her failing vision and increases her imaginative power. Ironically, she had earlier accused Rudolph of becoming too withdrawn and too detached; yet it is she who, finally, "frames" her husband on her perceptual canvas, a canvas that had earlier been blurred by her encroaching blindness. It is Rudolph, caught in mid-kick, who becomes the center of her vision, not the world, which she remains uncertain about.

The conclusions about aesthetics in "China" advance the same kind of privatization and isolation seen in the final pages of *Oxherding Tale*. Instead of developing the obvious intercultural strand of community in this story, Johnson develops Walter Pater's "art for art's sake" argument, which moves the notion of an unencumbered aesthetic process to the foreground. Because Johnson narrows the focus at the story's end to Evelyn's perspective and obsession with completing her own filmic narrative as artist, the story does not take full advantage of the links between art and community that Johnson develops elsewhere. Despite its limitations, for this collection "China" offers a possible cure to the despair that can affect African Americans worn down by existence in a racist society, as were the characters in "Exchange Value." Because of this, "China" is a powerful dramatization of some of Johnson's aesthetic notions, indicating again the close weave that binds his criticism, philosophy, spirituality, and fiction. The strands are ever coextensive. The tensions between them seem to perpetuate Johnson's fictional subjects and treatments.

3. Johnson, "Kwoon," 326.

Alethia

"China," when paired with "Alethia," offers the most familiar aesthetic and philosophical visions within *The Sorcerer's Apprentice*. Like Johnson's novels, both stories depict a triumphant and salvific movement from ignorance to wisdom, from despair to liberation. Originally published in 1979, "Alethia," like "China," shares much with *Oxherding Tale*. In many ways, it is an abbreviated or truncated version of that complex novel's statement of spiritual and philosophical aesthetics and social applications, albeit more ambiguously rendered.

In his lengthy examination of aesthetics in "The Origin of the Work of Art," Martin Heidegger helps to define the Greek term *aletheia*. Through art truth emerges. "For Greek thought the essence of knowing consists in *aletheia,* that is, in the revealing of beings." Aletheia refers to that ephiphanic moment in which truth is "unconcealed." It is, according to Heidegger, the magical and near mystical power of art to reveal or illuminate truth or being through the "opening up of a world." He writes, "Beings can be as beings only if they stand within and stand out within what is lighted in this lighting. Only this lighting grants and guarantees to us humans a passage to those beings that we ourselves are not, and access to the being that we ourselves are." The image of light, which figures so prominently in religious writings as a representation of the divine, as in, for instance, "Menagerie," has here been associated with the revelatory power of art. Interestingly, Heidegger's comments on art are strikingly similar to Johnson's in that he, too, grants art a special, nearly sacred power, and he emphasizes its intersubjective or integrative aspects as a "passage" providing access to others.[4]

From the very first paragraph, the story's narrator, an aging African American Chicago philosophy professor, documents his own evolution from a philosophical kinship to W. E. B. Du Bois to one to Jean Toomer, an African American writer strongly influenced by Eastern spirituality. In this movement, Johnson presents the narrative of his own aesthetic evolution, as he moved from a naturalist-informed attitude toward art into one informed more by Heidegger and the romantics, stressing the extraordinary place and possibilities of art. Despite his self-effacing comments that he is not a conjurer or artist, Johnson links him with the mystical achievement of Jean Toomer and of romantic thought in general through the story's climax.

4. Martin Heidegger, "The Origin of the Work of Art," 144–87.

In a familiar move, Johnson calls attention to transcendental love through his scholarly narrator, who suspects, perhaps too late in life, that the transcendence of relativism through love was truth. It is love that resolves the limitations of dualism, individuality, and their concomitant separation. Echoing Heidegger, the narrator realizes that alethia means "to call forth from concealedness" (*SA*, 103). Everyone is responsible for "conjuring only those visions from perceptual chaos that let be goodness, truth, beauty" (*SA*, 103). This traditional Platonic and romantic aesthetic is conjured forth in an act of artistic and philosophical creation (i.e., the act of imposing order on chaos). In a moralist spin reminiscent of the style of his mentor John Gardner, Johnson emphasizes the traditional moral function of art to convey beauty, truth, and goodness.

In this evocation of idealized and near Platonic Western aesthetics, race has not been erased. "Alethia" is important as a short story because it shows Johnson creating his own version of the Black Aesthetic. The professor's truth reveals that "*alethia* meant the celebration of exactly that ugly, lovely black life (so it was to me) I'd fled so long ago in my childhood" (*SA*, 104); he learns that it is his responsibility to see beauty in every aspect of that experience. This, he realizes, is the purpose of philosophy, to see, or to conjure beauty. Instead of fleeing blackness, his heritage, the narrator learns to see within it the particular and distinctive beauty it affords.

The professor's ruminations are prompted by a crisis in his career when a female student threatens to charge him with sexual harassment if he fails her. To avoid this charge he begins a relationship with the student, who takes him to a drug party at her apartment, where the professor experiences, in a scene reminiscent of *Oxherding Tale,* an integrative intimation of the Whole. In this drug-induced vision he realizes that the idea of an individual self or "I" is just a minimal part of endlessly changing black existence and community, which is itself endlessly complex and diverse in its inclusion of many different nationalities and perspectives. The professor thus replaces his notions of distinct individuality with an individual transcendence that connects him with a larger appreciation of the Whole in which the pretensions of selfhood fall away in the embrace of a larger universal design. This is his moment of alethia, or moment of unconcealed vision.

At first glance, this story would seem to be completely at odds with "Menagerie: A Child's Story," which emphasizes the breakdown and balkanization of American society rather than this mystical connectedness. Yet both "Alethia" and "Menagerie" posit the existence of a Platonic light from which all temporal forms originate. In "Menagerie," however, the unity is ignored and contradicted through what is presented as petty manifestations of essentialist individual and group desires, while in "Alethia," a drug vision leads to a deeper appreciation of the unity of all beings, particularly in the African American or black world.

In a revelatory and epiphanic vision that is itself an aesthetic experience, the professor, like Andrew Hawkins at the close of *Oxherding Tale*, sees the many manifestations of the Whole through different forms. This leads him to the realization that "in that evanescent, drugged instant, I did indeed desperately love her [the Whole]" (*SA*, 111). In a vision that repeats the underlying philosophy of "Menagerie," there is another dreamy vision of a "colorless light . . . so blinding it obliterated their outlines, blurred their precious differences, as if each were a rill of the same ancient light somehow imprisoned in form" (*SA*, 56); the universal shines from beneath individual difference in an expression of the formless original light. In "Menagerie" this spiritual emanation is self-destructively ignored; in "Alethia" the professor is unsure at the end of this very short story if he dreamed the vision of harmonious being or if he is dreaming his sense of differences. Yet, as a statement of Johnson's religious impulse and his idiosyncratic black aesthetic, "Alethia" is clearly the result and articulation of his by now familiar beliefs.

Entering the Abyss

The next story, "Popper's Disease," subverts the life-affirmation of Johnson's novels and some of his short stories like no other story in *The Sorcerer's Apprentice*. It is the climax of Johnson's despair. "Popper's Disease" is an angst-ridden interrogation of his most deeply held aesthetic, philosophical, and social beliefs—it is his journey into the abyss through the form of a science fiction fantasy set in the present.

Dr. Henry Popper, an African American, is married to a white woman. They live in a predominately white town in Illinois. He and his white neighbors avoid discussions of race, and they share a common Western cultural admiration for rationality and causality. In medical school he was the only African American student and so was called on to represent favorably all African Americans. Because of his difference, Popper doubts himself, and he wonders why his beautiful white wife married him. His successes as a doctor cannot alleviate the feeling that he has "not fully comprehended my own (foster) culture" (*SA*, 134). He is tormented by the feelings of "*thrownness* that every Negro experiences when hurled into a society that simultaneously supports and, I am saying, annihilates him" (*SA*, 134).

Through this story Johnson inverts his own beliefs. For example, in *Being and Race,* Johnson states that "the actor and writer—and all of us really—believe in the interchangeability standpoints; we throw ourselves *with* a character toward his projects" (*BR,* 43). The artistic strategy that Johnson touts in his critical writing as a path to potential liberation is subverted in "Popper's Disease" through his main character's feelings of profound displacement and racial alienation living in the white world.

Neither are Popper's feelings ever alleviated. While on his way to visit a patient in the country, he is confronted with a flying saucer, which may, as Popper is aware, be one of the "psychic phenomena, products of a troubled mind broken by peering too long at the abyss" (*SA,* 132). Hearing a squeal from within the strange ship, and feeling that his services as a doctor are needed, Popper enters it and is immediately immersed in a completely different perceptual universe, in which Western distinctions of up, down, left, and right appear to have no meaning. The pilot, a bizarre refraction of Popper's racial dilemma, greets him and reveals that his culture has exiled him until a cure for his disease can be discovered. Like Popper, the creature is tortured by a debilitating ambivalence toward the dominant culture, which has a certain beauty and appeal and yet is poised to destroy him because of his difference. These feelings, explains the creature, have "led other Plague victims to irascibility, violence, moodiness, a morbid fascination with Time, boredom . . . and, worst of all, thermogenesis [internal combustion]" (*SA,* 138). The malady, as Popper had identified earlier when considering the damaging impact of culture on health, is located in a maddeningly intangible realm of cultural perspective.

Popper's anxieties over difference are depicted on the ship's Telecipher. There he sees his wife and a young white male having sex and mocking Popper. This vision intensifies Popper's feelings of inadequacy and leads him to despair. Interrupting his self-flagellation, the creature realizes that all his perceptions are the result of his ego. This phenomenological and Buddhist insight, which, for other characters in Johnson's fictions would be a source of comfort and potential release, is, for Popper, evidence that the creature—and Popper—are justified in their pessimistic perceptions about their futures.

The creature dies, leaving Popper trapped inside the spaceship, quarantined by the military just as the creature had been quarantined by his own culture. Popper spends months reviewing information on the Telecipher, realizing that he may be peering, again, into a fantastic representation of his own broken mind. Popper, in his explorations, glimpses an alternative historical time, centuries before Peking Man, a time when "Dualism was death" (*SA,* 144)—an Edenic time of holistic, harmonious existence between individuals and races.

Popper programs the Telecipher to decipher the creature's science and discovers it is based on quantum field theory, which creates a mystical field that is "Continuous in time, everywhere in space, the field was the idea of polymorphy made fact" (*SA,* 144). To Popper, this unified and holistic vision resembles a powerful alternative to Western dualism, one that dissolves distinctions and recognizes the existence of an underlying universal Being that takes temporary shape in different, transient and, therefore, inessential guises. This theme of an alternate, holistic reality, so positively presented in his novels, seems to take on a different coloring in his short stories, where it is part of a nightmarish experience that can never be completely deciphered or attained.

When the Telecipher begins to diagnose the pilot's disease, Popper is interrupted by his wife, Mildred, and the mayor of his town calling to him from outside the spaceship. They want to know if the space creatures are dead, and if so, why. Popper, aware that as a mistrusted minority he must swear by his diagnosis, waits for the Telecipher's answer. In the control room Popper reads the screen, which is like looking into a mirror of his own thoughts: "*It's the Self* and *There is no cure*" (*SA,* 146).

While "Popper's Disease" shares a perspective that emphasizes holism and universality with "China" and *Oxherding Tale,* it reverses their conclusion. Instead of being liberated or comforted by his exposure to this alternate mode of perception, Popper simply recognizes the extent and cause of his own mental disease. Popper, unlike Andrew in *Oxherding Tale* or Rudolph in "China," remains isolated at the end of the story, trapped inside a horrifying version of his own fears and racial discontents. Whereas Andrew draws nearer to his white wife in pursuit of dharma as a householder at the end of the novel, and Rudolph and Evelyn become reconciled and reinvigorated, the doctor in "Popper's Disease" remains alienated from his white neighbors and his white wife and ever more acutely aware of his own difference and separation from his foster culture. When the gods display to Faith their sign in "In This Sign Conjure" (*F,* 191), Faith's quest is in some way resolved. For Popper, there is no such affirmation.

It is as if Johnson used "Popper's Disease" to explore the horrific aspects of assimilation, extending the skepticism seen in "The Education of Mingo," to equate assimilation and integration for African Americans with annihilation, negation, and disease. What makes "Popper's Disease" distinctive, however, is how Johnson takes the very same ideas about self and society that have comforted, consoled, and cured his characters in other works and alters the perspective to yield a bleaker portrait of contemporary ethnic identity.

Anxiety of Influence: Johnson and John Gardner

In the title story of the collection, "The Sorcerer's Apprentice," published first in 1982, Johnson returns to the themes he emphasized in the "The Education of Mingo." Like several of the stories in this collection, this one does not provide a magic and optimistic cure for the social, racial, and internal dilemmas that vex its characters. In "The Sorcerer's Apprentice," Johnson reflexively looks further into the abyss of the artist's self-doubt and struggle for originality than in any other of his works, using this story to reflect on his own apprenticeship relationship with early mentor, teacher, and creative writer John Gardner as well as his pervasive aesthetic strategy of integrative inclusion of intertextual sources.

"The Sorcerer's Apprentice" begins with a master conjurer or magician named Rubin in search of an apprentice to teach before he dies. From the generation of men who still remember African spiritualism, Rubin chooses a boy who loves and admires the sorcerer figure, "especially the effects of his craft, which comforted the sick, held back evil, and blighted the enemies of newly freed slaves with locusts and bad health" (*SA*, 149). As in *Faith and the Good Thing*, African American conjuring is a subversive force, powerful enough to counter the reigning white racist power hierarchy and to preserve a historical connection with generations past.

The connection Johnson makes with aesthetics in "The Sorcerer's Apprentice" is clear. As a craft, sorcery or conjuring is imbued with a life-affirming, moral force—it can hold back evil and comfort the sick. Allan Jackson, the apprentice, admires in Rubin his power to do good and also his artistic mastery. The apprentice tells Rubin that he plans to work hard to understand and replicate the tonalities of his mentor's voice as he conjures. Allan sees in Rubin's skills not only racial empowerment and historical connectedness, but also access to a rich and empowering aesthetic heritage to which Rubin is privy.

The naive apprentice is frustrated at first that his master does not immediately reveal all his secrets. As a fledgling magician, he longs for immediate, miraculous wisdom, but instead he is given menial tasks that seem to have nothing to do with sorcery. Rubin cautions his pupil against being too faithful or too eager, since overzealousness may turn magic's power to do good into evil. As an experienced artist or conjurer, Rubin knows that "White magic comes and goes" (*SA*, 151) and that the magic of inspiration is fundamentally unpredictable.

Despite his initial frustration, Allan is a quick study and is soon performing entertaining exhibits of ventriloquism and levitation. Allan's learning parallels Johnson's learning from Gardner. What Johnson, initially, wants to learn from Gardner is "his prodigious understanding of technique, his gift for voice and narrative ventriloquism . . . achieved in nearly perfect pitch in fully cadenced, poetic lines that seamlessly fused image and idea." Similarly, Allan hopes to hear in Rubin's techniques and narrative voice the secrets of conjuring the voices of his African ancestors. Through deep study Allan realizes the integrative nature of art: that these conjuring spells are a product of the African American community as a whole and cannot be owned by any one person. This realization allays Allan's anxiety that the spells seem permeated by the sorcerer's personality exclusively and do not come from himself.[5]

Despite this realization, however, the anxiety of influence grows. The part of Allan's talent for conjuring that seems most original and independent of his teacher is that about which he is least confident. As his ability grows, so does his uncertainty. He is able to cure people with his miraculous spells, but the sorcerer can do that, and Allan's insecurity is greatest when "the compliments compared a fledgling wizard to other magicians, as if the apprentice had achieved nothing new, or on his own" (*SA*, 156). Allan, as sorcerer and artist, feels as if he has no control over his magical inspiration and is merely a temporary medium for whatever power, or magical text, flies through him. These anxieties culminate in the feeling that if he, as conjurer/artist is overly dependent on the will of the spell, then he is essentially a conduit. To combat these feelings of impotence, Allan dedicates himself to mastering the many strategies and techniques from his mentor that will allow him to do good.

His self-serving and survivalistic strategy of imitation and devotion to technique downplay the significance of inspiration and originality and will protect him when his conjuring magic disappears. His strategy places him in the curious position of distrusting the success of his first attempt at healing. The unpredictability and ephemerality of artistic inspiration undermines Allan's confidence. He learns what Moses Green in "The Education of Mingo" realizes only after watching his "creation," Mingo, turn his ideas and inspiration into murder and destruction.

After mastering these conjuring techniques, Allan realizes that he has no more to learn from Rubin and feels that he has graduated to the level of sorcerer. At the height of his powers, Allan is admired and celebrated in his town. Yet, he still wonders (making explicit the connection between sorcery and writing), "Was sorcery a gift given to a few, like poetry?"

5. Gardner, "Introduction to *On Writers*," xi.

(*SA*, 158). If this is true, if inspiration is externally given, then, he realizes, his career as a sorcerer is over. Wallowing in self-doubt, Allan realizes that he was not born into the magical Allmuseri tribe, as Rubin was. All he has, he realizes, is "a vast and painfully acquired yet hollow repertoire of tricks" (*SA*, 159). These tricks could allow him to be a facile entertainer, but they would never allow him to do the kind of moral good that Rubin achieved when he successfully defeated evil and healed the sick. Rubin embodies Gardner's critical expectations for art, including fiction, that it be life affirming, life-giving, and essentially moral.

Allan's abilities are soon put to the test. His father takes him home, where a woman has brought her dying baby, who refuses to eat. Allan begins by drawing upon the thousands of techniques he has amassed during his apprenticeship. These "dazzling array of devices" so closely mimic the sorcerer that "it seemed that Rubin, not Allan, worked magic in the room" (*SA*, 163). But, because he is not the sorcerer, the spells seem only to have a negative effect. The baby starts spitting blood and then lapses into a coma. The sorcerer's initial warning about the dangers of being too faithful and too eager as an imitative apprentice have turned into prophecy. In an echo of "The Education of Mingo," the creative good that Allan hoped to accomplish through his art has turned into its antithesis.

Faced with humiliating failure, Allan contemplates suicide through the spell of last resort, which Rubin warned him against. This ultimate spell calls forth the demons of artistic self-doubt and impotence from the river. On his walk to the river, Allan gazes into this chasm of despair, thinking that his white magic was flawed and ultimately imitative: "His talent was for pa(o)stiche. He could imitate but never truly heal; impress but never conjure beauty; ape the good but never again give rise to a genuine spell" (*SA*, 164–5). While he has mastered the sorcerer's techniques and strategies, he has not become a genuine sorcerer, able to create beauty and perform good on his own, according to romantic ideals of the individual artist. His myriad techniques of parody and pastiche seem mere imitative exercises in intertextual genre-crossing virtuosity instead of genuine art. Instead of order, beauty, and inspiration that define the genuine spell (or art), Allan feels only absence and the accompanying feelings of emptiness and sterility. In this nadir of depression, Allan feels that it would have been better never to have attempted a spell than to have hidden his incompetence with flashy and superficial aesthetic techniques.

In invoking these demons, Allan opens up an aesthetic hell and accepts despair and damnation. Once invoked, the demons only echo and intensify his own feelings of inadequacy and incompetence as an original conjurer and mere parodic imitator. They mock him for making Rubin's once good and beautiful spells into monstrosities, turning what was white magic into black magic. They identify parody as his chief sin. Allan then realizes the true destructiveness of his aspirations, ruing the effect that his parasitic work has caused.

In this story Johnson dramatizes the problem of aesthetic apprenticeship and mentorship. Despite the best intentions the imitative artist can turn what was originally good and for the good into a disfigured monstrosity. The act of mimicry, or intertextual pastiche, at first empowering and entertaining, quickly turns on the apprentice and leads to loss of spontaneous inspiration and a reliance on dazzling, but ultimately hollow, effect. More than this, the very spells learned from his teacher are ultimately unpredictable: in different contexts and from a different source, they can be destructive.

This story seems to affirm Gardner's initial premise that art can do good or evil, that it can be used for moral purposes. He writes, "I have claimed that art is essentially and primarily moral—that is, life-giving—moral in its process of creation and moral in what it says." Further, claims Gardner, art destroys evil through its inspiring example. It holds up order and moral principles against the chaos and moral wasteland of the world. If it does not, then it is not worthy of being called art. Yet in both "The Education of Mingo," and "The Sorcerer's Apprentice," Johnson counters Gardner's confidence about the preserving and controlling power of art by showing how art and aesthetic production can go awry in unexpected and unpredictable ways that are essentially self-destructive. In his introductory homage to Gardner from *On Writers and Writing*, Johnson quotes from one of Gardner's televised appearances, in which he talked confidently about attaining a kind of control over the universe through creating a convincing fictional character. This control, one assumes, becomes part of the moral method and message that Gardner emphasizes as one of the premier functions of high literary art. Perhaps Johnson wrote "The Sorcerer's Apprentice" to work through lingering differences with his nearly overpowering mentor. His conclusions in this and other stories in the collection disprove Gardner's point about control and predictability— recall "Menagerie," for instance—and call into question Gardner's emphasis on narrative ventriloquism and the appropriation and blending of old literary forms. Johnson is using his stories, especially "The Sorcerer's Apprentice," both to pay homage to Gardner and to distance himself from Gardner's "white magic," while interrogating some of his own most deeply held beliefs about aesthetics and inspiration.[6]

6. Gardner, *On Moral Fiction,* 15; Gardner, "Introduction to *On Writers,*" ix.

Johnson critiques Gardner's rigid moralistic certainty about the role and purpose of art directly and indirectly in all these short stories. "The Education of Mingo" and "The Sorcerer's Apprentice" reject Gardner's programmatic assertions by illustrating the chaotic, monstrous, and uncontrollable results of artistic creation. Attempts to enact Gardner's rigid determinations about art result in "distorted shadows" ("The Education of Mingo") and monstrous disfigurations. Yet the fact that Johnson spends so much time disproving Gardner illustrates the extent to which Johnson is still deeply involved in an intertextual conversation with Gardner's aesthetics and legacy. Even recently, Johnson has written a reflection on Gardner's lasting influence in "John Gardner as Mentor." In the article Johnson states, "But even the best of literary apprenticeships, those based on love and mutual respect, can have drawbacks. The elder artist, if his personality and gifts are as strong as Gardner's were, may have problems with new directions his student may take"—a statement referring to the heated disagreements they had over Eastern religion in *Oxherding Tale,* also published in 1982.[7]

"The Sorcerer's Apprentice" does not end with Allan's suicide, even though his conjuring failures have driven him to the brink of suicide. Had the collection ended with Allan's suicide, the themes of monstrosity, social meltdown, and African American despair would have taken precedence over the muted chords of renewal and vitality within the collection, especially evident in "China." Instead, Allan chooses to step away from suicide toward his father, who has accompanied him to the river. Allan erases the chalk circle he had inscribed in the dirt to invoke the demons and steps away. Symbolically, he has broken the vicious cycle of mentorship and apprenticeship and returned to his family, to his waiting and loving father, whom he had striven so hard to please. In breaking the cycle, Allan feels "within his chest the first spring of resignation, a giving way of both the hunger to heal and the anxiety to avoid evil" (*SA,* 168). Thus he lets go of his desire to follow Rubin's teachings and embraces an alternative vision, a Zen Buddhist vision that stresses resignation and the elimination of ego—the same strategy that earlier cured Rudolph's illness and had, in *Oxherding Tale,* allowed, via Reb's inspirational example, for Andrew's physical and spiritual release. No longer what Rubin expected him to be, Allan does not know how to comfort or please his father—the teacher behind the teacher. Instead of spells, words, or magically drawn circles, Allan's connection with his father is physical. He squeezes "the old man's thick, ruined fingers" (*SA,* 168), and his father, previously distant,

7. "John Gardner," 623.

falls toward him. This unity of father and son drives away the demons and triumphs over the evil of their self-imposed distance. At the story's end Allan has replaced Rubin, the father-substitute or surrogate, with his original father and learned the depth and sustenance of his love.

As he did in *Oxherding Tale*, Johnson offers the solution of the reconciliation with the father as the first step toward healing and growth. In that final squeeze of his father's fingers is a recognition of the artistry and aesthetics of his father's life as he sacrificed his own life to support his family, during which he subjected his body to the endless punishment of hard physical labor. Instead of being "fugitives with no fingers" (*SA*, 19), as are Moses and Mingo, unable to create or to hope, Allan and his father form a tight connection through their fingers—this becomes the magical empowerment, a repetition of Faith's final life-artistry that may heal them and bring them closer together not so much through art or conjuration, but through a humble human connection. This gesture may begin to resolve, in an extremely private and individual way, the internal and external dilemmas of African American experience and identity that accumulate in this short story collection. If it does not resolve the problems of the racial abyss, at least this relationship can provide some recuperative consolation and empowerment.

In casting off the influence of Gardner's white magic, Johnson returns to an empowering and humbling Zen Buddhist surrender of desire, ambition, and fear and a consequential redefinition of the aesthetic toward life-artistry and empowerment through love and the originary African American family fragmented by slavery's toxic legacy. This first step toward the loss or annihilation of the self and its ego-desires may perhaps reverse the pessimistic conclusion of "Popper's Disease," when he's told, "*It's the self* and *There is no cure*" (*SA*, 146).

In a previously unpublished story, "The Gift of the *Osuo*," Johnson explores many of the themes he uses in the other stories, yet this time by examining cartooning. In this compressed Buddhist fairy tale, the African King Shabaka is given a piece of magic chalk. Drawings made with it come to life. The king gets carried away by this wizardry and creates a spectacular array of figures and wealth for his Allmuserian kingdom. The narrator comments, "[T]here was no mimesis here: Shabaka's animals resembled, not the Real, but the Real transfigured (which is the origin of all beauty, all art)." King Shabaka becomes the romantic artist, who imposes his artistic will on reality, transforming it into his idealized perception. Even if his aesthetic vision is "physically wrong, it was poetically right." In a Gardnerian move, King Shabaka uses his artistic power to defeat his enemies, hold back evil, and create good for his kingdom. And yet, in a familiar dynamic, the artistic power overpowers its conjuring practitioner—when the chalk runs out the very images that had held the entire country spellbound now turn against him and his people. The king is trapped with the "malodorous images of all he had wished for and willed in his lifetime." These cartoonish images are "like crustaceans that he could not brush away." Interestingly they have become fixed, and rigidified, as if Johnson were, again, commenting on the limitations of the static cartooning image, as he does in the denouement of *Oxherding Tale*. Soon he, his son, and the rest of the Allmuseri are either slaughtered or enslaved by a neighboring tribe. Like Allan, King Shabaka realizes almost too late that the desire to create—to impose one's desires and projections upon the world through art—is inherently dangerous and destructive. As the king waits to be sold the next morning, he realizes, "He had acted to end hunger, need, want, and—behold—each act of the ego engendered suffering."[8]

"The Gift of the *Osuo*" turns from fairy tale to heavy-handed parable when the king awakens from what, it turns out, has all been a nightmare. One of the tribe's wizards lectures the king and cautions him against imposing his desires on the world, urging instead a Buddhist "maximum concern for life, but minimum attachment." Thus the story ends on a resounding note against the ego-projection and romantic transfigurations that shape artistic creations, thereby severing the connection between the artistic and the social. An early artistic effort, "The Gift of the *Osuo*" demonstrates Johnson's pre-*Oxherding Tale* thinking; there is a clear separation between the aesthetic impulse and the health of the community or nation-state. The king, like Allan, has survived his experiment with artistic and aesthetic vanity and authorship only by realizing the hollowness and emptiness of individual aesthetic desire. Even given Johnson's aesthetic evolution, which will be explored more fully in the chapter on *Middle Passage*, Johnson's moralizing impetus seems to be to urge against the aesthetic impulse—the very impulse that creates the narrative tensions and materials for his fiction. In their assertions and negations, Johnson's most complex fictions about aesthetics resembles the dizzying convolutions of a Mobius strip.[9]

As Allan in "The Sorcerer's Apprentice" recognizes, he will have to live waiting for the inspiration to conjure that may, conceivably, never grace him again. Art, which is the self's expression, depends on the very desires and hungers that, in taking the first step toward Zen Buddhist

8. Charles Johnson, "The Gift of the *Osuo*," 521, 523, 525, 526.
9. Ibid., 526.

self-abnegation and quiescence, Allan jettisons. This artless result is, however, one of the few aspects of Johnson's aesthetics that *The Sorcerer's
Apprentice* does not explicitly interrogate. Although understandable, it is
ironic that Johnson creates some of his most haunting and vivid artistic
products through his fictive warnings against the validity and morality of
the aesthetic impulse. Johnson's art contains the simultaneous double-
gesture of exploitation and denial, of assertion and withdrawl.

Conclusions

As a collection, *The Sorcerer's Apprentice* stands as ironic commentary
on the novels, challenging Johnson's most cherished and characteristic
assumptions about identity, art, and authorship. Many of these stories call
into question the validity of Johnson's integrative and assimilative cultural
and social vision, at times even seeming to proffer arguments in favor of
ethnocentrism and the maintenance of a protected racial identity, as in
"The Education of Mingo" or, perhaps, "Popper's Disease," as means
of survival in the face of pervasive white racism and oppression. Compellingly, integrationism is, at times, equated with cultural and individual
annihilation as several characters are trapped in the echoing cavern of
their own diseased minds, isolated from themselves and others as they
struggle, unsuccessfully, to maintain their sanity. The psychological and
economic conditions of African American life have seldom been rendered
more vividly through so many genre variations.

At the same time, some of the stories reflect Johnson's integrative
and religiously informed ideological and political solutions, albeit largely
through negative implication, as in "Menagerie: A Child's Fable." The
author of these stories *is* the same one who will write *Middle Passage,* and
yet there is a profound and powerful difference. Perhaps freed from the
dictates of writing "responsible fiction," which emphasizes life-affirmation
and the triumph over suffering, Johnson is free to plumb the limitations
of his ideology and aesthetics at the deepest and most revealing substrata.
It is as if Johnson's short stories hold up a fractured mirror to the positive
holistic denouements of his novels. Because of this, the short stories often
resonate with more power, depth, and ambiguity than his longer works.
Throughout *Middle Passage,* as we shall explore, Johnson succeeds in
transferring his esoteric ideas about spirituality and philosophy to an easily
accessible and fast-paced, plot-driven examination of North American
society without the angst-ridden reflexivity so marvelously achieved in
his collection of short stories.

5

Revisions of Self and Society

Middle Passage and *Invisible Man*

When Johnson won the National Book Award for *Middle Passage* in 1990, his acceptance speech was an opportunity for him to lavish praise on Ralph Ellison, whose aesthetic precedent and vision had long inspired Johnson. Ellison was in the audience to hear the speech that honored him while hinting at Johnson's initial ideological distance from him. When Johnson first read *Invisible Man* during the Black Arts movement of the late sixties his response was somewhat limited: "it wasn't until years later in the 1970s, after I'd taught *Invisible Man* several times, that I began to fully appreciate the intellectual expansiveness and artistic generosity of his novel."[1]

His account of reading *Invisible Man* for the first time has a different shading in an article written for *The Washington Post* soon after Ellison's death. Johnson recalls that he spent "three memorable nights . . . being altered by his remarkable adventure of ideas and artistic possibility" even though he read the book in an "anti-intellectual climate thick with separatist arguments . . . when both Ellison and poet Robert Hayden were snubbed by those under the spell of black cultural nationalism." In this article, written three years after the National Book Award speech, Johnson seems to separate himself from those critics who snubbed Ellison to emphasize the novel's transformative effect on him. Even though Johnson "came of age" during this time, he seems more limited as an appreciative reader by his own inexperience than by his politics.[2]

1. Charles Johnson, "National Book Award Acceptance Speech," 208–9.
2. Charles Johnson, "The Singular Vision of Ralph Ellison," C4.

135

Middle Passage is Johnson's 1990s homage to Ellison's influence and achievement. As Johnson stated in a 1994 group interview, which included Amiri Baraka, Leon Forrest, and Gwendolyn Brooks, receiving the National Book Award was "a moment that I'd lived for, I think, as a writer—to be able to stand in front of the world and talk about what I think is one of our most important novels by a black man of the 20th century." Johnson, like Ellison before him, creates an intellectual African American narrator who journeys through history meeting a broad spectrum of characters and sets him in a story that blends humor and suspense. Similar to the ending of *Invisible Man,* where the narrator makes Emersonian pronouncements about the nature of American democracy, *Middle Passage* ends with Rutherford Calhoun, the narrator of *Middle Passage,* reaching conclusions about being an American citizen. As he has done before with different texts, Johnson folds Ellison's novel into his own, integrating and extending its vision.[3]

Johnson's self-effacing National Book Award acceptance speech, which spends more time on Ellison's work than on his own achievement, might lead readers to overestimate the influence of *Invisible Man* on *Middle Passage.* Johnson's novel is markedly different from Ellison's in its conclusions about self and society. Whereas *Invisible Man* leaves its anonymous narrator in a state of isolated modernist alienation, *Middle Passage* dramatizes the interrelatedness and complexities of human community, even for African Americans victimized by slavery.

Middle Passage represents a new phase in Johnson's evolving aesthetics. Unlike his earlier novels, *Middle Passage* is a direct and extended examination of the strengths and weaknesses of United States society. Johnson applies his Eastern-inspired conclusions about individual identity to the broader canvas of society. Unlike his approach in "Menagerie: A Child's Fable" and "The Education of Mingo," Johnson blends the political, the spiritual, and the aesthetic into a seamless life-affirming whole. In his final phase (which will include *Dreamer*), Johnson creates literature that does not differentiate between the private and the public, the artistic and the political. Johnson completes the move he began at the end of *Oxherding Tale* by applying his spiritual imagination to the state of the nation.

East Meets West

In *Middle Passage* Johnson goes back to the beginning of African American history to treat the horrors of the Middle Passage, the second stage of

3. "Remembering Ralph Ellison," 37.

a triangular trade route between England, Africa, and the Americas. For reasons not yet fully explored by scholars, there have been few extended literary treatments of this traumatic event in African American history. Robert Hayden's poem, "Middle Passage" (1966), Amiri Baraka's play *Slave Ship. A Historical Pageant* (1967), Alex Haley's *Roots* (1976), and, more recently, Toni Morrison's *Beloved* (1988) are the primary exceptions.

A quick comparison of Johnson's *Middle Passage* with Morrison's *Beloved* reveals their differences and similarities as writers. Johnson and Morrison's treatment of the historical event includes historically accurate description of the brutalities endured: the confinement, the violent abuse, the disease, revolts, death, and inhuman conditions. Yet, where Johnson will treat the Middle Passage primarily as a metaphor for integrationism, Morrison uses the experience as primarily a touchstone of psychic disintegration and unendurable, or unspeakable anguish. Repressed memories of the nearly unspeakable event surface periodically in the "Beloved" sections of Morrison's novel: "I do not eat the men without skin bring us their morning water to drink we have none at night I cannot see the dead man on my face." This gruesome detail becomes part of the unendurable weight of the collective racial past that helps to precipitate the hallucinatory violence and despair that pervades the novel.[4]

In "Rootedness: The Ancestor as Foundation," Morrison identifies key features of African American writing, including the presence or absence of the ancestor figure. "There is always an elder there," writes Morrison. "And these ancestors are not just parents, they are sort of timeless people whose relationship to the characters are benevolent, instructive, and protective, and they provide a certain kind of wisdom." Yet Baby Suggs, *Beloved*'s primary spiritual ancestor, collapses after the accumulated horrors of the Middle Passage and slavery become too much. Baby Suggs is well known for taking care of the community, for her preaching and her love, and for her ability to heal the sick. But her holy, ancestral powers are destroyed by her daughter-in-law Sethe's traumatic experiences. When Sethe kills one of her babies with a handsaw to protect it from slavery, "Her faith, her love, her imagination and her great big old heart began to collapse twenty-eight days after her daughter-in-law arrived," and she spends the rest of her life passively studying colors. Finally, for Baby Suggs, "the sadness was at her center, the desolated center where the self that was no self made its home." Without this anchoring ancestor figure, other characters experience psychological breakdowns: one character thinks "because she has no self . . . She can feel her thickness thinning, dissolving

4. Toni Morrison, *Beloved*, 210.

into nothing," and Sethe lapses into episodes of madness and delusional dreams of revenge.[5]

Johnson treats many of these same themes—yet the accumulation of horror and the disintegration of self have surprisingly different results. Instead of being psychically destroyed by his experience and further separated from his ancestors, Johnson's African American narrator and artist-figure, Rutherford Calhoun, experiences an empowering Buddhist loss of self. His painful, inadvertent participation in the Middle Passage experience paradoxically reconnects him with his African ancestors as an integral part of his heritage. As is characteristic of Johnson's quest narratives, in this story Rutherford must first confront and live through one of the most painful and traumatic experiences of African American history and then immerse himself in new ways of experiencing the world before achieving some degree of personal and spiritual contentment.

At the end of the first chapter Rutherford, a recently freed man of color, who is interested only in satisfying his immediate sensual desires to make up for years of enslavement, stows away on the nearest ship docked in the New Orleans harbor to escape gambling debts and the prospect of getting married. Rutherford, witness to one of the most profoundly alienating moments of cultural displacement, ironically, soon becomes a synthetic merger of East and West. Through his ordeals, Rutherford learns the fundamental truths of Buddhism and recognizes the limitations of the Western pursuit of the very sensual desires that propelled him at the beginning of the narrative.

Initially, life on the ship the *Republic* is portrayed as one of extremes between East and West. At the beginning of the story, the ship is headed for the West Coast of Africa to pick up forty enslaved Allmuseri and some valuable material goods. The *Republic* is captained by a monomaniacal figure, Captain Ebenezer Falcon, a dwarf, whose name suggests the American eagle and whose characterization directly recalls Melville's Captain Ahab. Taken to the captain by members of the crew after he is discovered, Rutherford sees Falcon as a representative caricature of Western past. He is the quintessential colonialist exploiter. Johnson uses Falcon to run roughshod over Johnson's most cherished beliefs by, for example, stealing sacred scrolls from Buddhist temples in Tibet.

Despite his revulsion at what Falcon has done and what he represents, Rutherford seems awed by Falcon and his exploits. As the book's initial "artist" or ship's log keeper, Falcon may represent the artist Rutherford

5. Toni Morrison, "Rootedness: The Ancestor as Foundation," 343; *Beloved*, 89, 140, 123.

needs to replace or supplant in order to achieve spiritual contentment and peace. Just as Falcon, through his obsessions, brings Rutherford close to death, he bequeaths to Rutherford a salvific path when he asks Rutherford to be his biographer and historian of the events on the ship. It is only at the end of the novel, when Rutherford is recovering aboard the *Juno*, which rescues him after the *Republic* sinks, that he is able to pour out his feelings. In the logbook, he reconstructs the narrative chronologically, first as a way to alleviate some of the trauma and pain of his experiences and then to achieve something else. In the beginning, he merely records the events, but then Rutherford feels the need to "transfigure" his experience by making it something greater than a realistic account. As with the other artist-figures in Johnson's fiction, Rutherford achieves liberation from the realism of his past by transforming it into an artistically ordered product. Through Rutherford's movement from pain-filled realism to a spiritually enriched poeticism, Johnson transcribes his own movement as a writer who, with *Faith and the Good Thing,* transcended his own apprentice novels dedicated primarily to mimicking the forms of realism and naturalism.

Through his dramatization of writing and artistry, Johnson covertly returns to some familiar themes about aesthetics. Although the logic of having Rutherford's log predate Falcon's death is never fully explained, it seems clear that Johnson wanted to create a traditional narrative, with a tightly unified plot comprising a clear beginning, middle, and end. Rutherford's mystical and erudite log replaces Falcon's brooding, monomaniacal, and lonely log entries so characteristic of his perfectionist perspective. On one level Johnson may be delving again—as in "The Sorcerer's Apprentice"—into his autobiographical and literary relationship with John Gardner through Rutherford's/Johnson's Eastern replacement of Falcon's/Gardner's predominately Western perspective, while on another he is still voicing an indebtedness to Falcon/Gardner for launching Rutherford's/Johnson's "literary" career. Rutherford replaces Falcon's journals, which contain evidence of a doomed discontent caused by the "twisted will of Puritanism" (*MP*, 51), with his own entries, which evolve into an optimistic meditation on Eastern spirituality and its applications for individual and social contentment.

There is a paradox in Rutherford's artistry, however, that repeats the deepest self-reflexive moments in his short stories. The novel, like *Ox-herding Tale,* is deeply informed, as we will soon discuss, by Buddhist doctrine. Yet Rutherford's artistic efforts are word-bound. His transformations do not have the same spiritual power as those of life-artists Faith or Imani, who engage in aesthetic production without the need for any particular canvas or artistic product. In Buddhism there is a deep distrust of words and intellectual debate, as this ninth-century poem from Buddhist scripture makes clear. "The whole world is tormented by words / And there is no one who does without words. / But in so far as one is free from words / Does one really understand words." Once Rutherford achieves his enlightenment, his narrative ends. As with Allan in "The Sorcerer's Apprentice," Rutherford finds that his artistic desire ends as he cleanses or purges himself through the act of artistic creation. Johnson's attempt to interject Eastern spirituality into daily American life through his writings carries with it the Mobius-strip logic of assertion and retraction, affirmation and negation. Paradoxically, Johnson pushes readers toward a rejection of words through words. Certainly it is through words— or the act of writing—that Rutherford reaches the state of quiescence necessary to stop writing and pursue his own spiritual development. A central, repeated paradox in Johnson's work is that it advocates for its own silence or ending. Unlike "The Sorcerer's Apprentice," and, to some extent, "The Gift of the *Osuo*," this narrative of self-reflexive interrogation remains beneath the surface of the narrative and can only be accessed through a familiarity with the intricate dance that appears in Johnson's earlier works about aesthetics, influence, and philosophical and spiritual perspectives.[6]

Yet there are surface manifestations of this allegory, especially in Rutherford's attitude toward his mentor. When Falcon attempts to shock Rutherford by talking about cannibalism and eating an African of whom Rutherford reminds him, Rutherford recognizes a familiar delight in narrating stories and feeding his egoistic desires for stimulation and excitement. As Falcon's eager apprentice, Rutherford uses his narrative— which describes in horrific detail his adventures—to evoke a range of responses from his audience, revealing his and Falcon's "desire to be fascinating objects in the eyes of others" (*MP*, 33). Despite extreme differences, both characters have a Western-oriented desire to feed their own egos through their narrative powers. It is only through the process of writing, at first in response to these desires and then beyond them, that Rutherford recreates himself and distances himself from Falcon's Western romantic-artist model.

The subject of Rutherford's log, the ship itself, becomes a philosophically charged and subtle symbol of Rutherford's aesthetic process. In its improvised, patchwork design, Rutherford sees an endless maze of complexity and instability. Instead of being fixed, static, or certain, the

6. Edward Conze, *Buddhist Scriptures*, 177.

ship is pure process, "perpetually flying apart and re-forming" (*MP*, 36). On another level, the ship is a symbol of the United States' identity; it represents the nation's act of perpetual, willful self-recreation as a joint communal project. Through the vehicle of the ship Johnson stresses the socially applicable tenor—the integrationist, interdependent, and mutual nature of the successful social enterprise, which, before it can be successful, must adopt and adapt to new ways of seeing.

There is another level of allegory relating to aesthetics. One ship must first sink before Rutherford can liberate himself from his own aesthetic and artistic constrictions. His movement at the end of the narrative from the *Republic* to the *Juno* is replete with significance. The "republic," or the Greek conception of society, is replaced by roman mythology: Juno was the sister and wife of Jupiter, queen of the gods and goddess of marriage. *Middle Passage* shows a narrative evolution similar to but hidden more deeply than that in *Faith and the Good Thing;* naturalistic and realist "forms" are replaced, or supplanted by superior antirealist mythopoetic modes. While *Middle Passage* certainly treats the integrative society more fully than any previous novel, it contains a hidden gesture toward the mythopoesis of *Faith and the Good Thing* and repeats the movement toward the spiritualized domestic tranquility achieved at the end of *Oxherding Tale.*

The Romantic Imagination

Johnson uses the symbol of the ocean to further his romantic celebration of the uncontained and unpredictable imagination, unconstrained by any predictable ideological platform. Those more tied to Western modes of perception are deeply threatened by the mystery, chaos, and immensity of the ocean. On the one hand a romantic myth embodying escape from domesticity and everyday responsibilities, the ocean is, on the other, threatening in its wildness and unpredictability. The first mate, a New England Brahmin, is terrified by what he sees as only chaos and disorder. Although he has been a seaman all his life, he is, unexpectedly, threatened by what he calls "that thrashing Void called the Atlantic" (*MP*, 36). The *Republic* and its attendant Western laws are constantly threatened with annihilation by the indifferent, thrashing ocean beneath.

This view of nature is a Western one, since the Buddhist notion of the void is quite different and does not contain the same ominous, threatening overtones. As Buddhist scholar Hajimi Nakamura relates, "The Void is all-inclusive; having no opposite, there is nothing which it excludes or opposes. It is living void, because all forms come out of it, and whoever realizes this void is filled with life . . . and the love of all beings." While this living void is empty, it is the paradoxical and essential full emptiness of Nirvana and the Body of Essence of the Buddha. Johnson seems to borrow directly from these ideas, since he has Rutherford describe the ocean as a nearly supernatural force, in which "form [is] superimposed upon form" and "endlessly spawned all creatures conceivable yet never consumed itself" (*MP*, 79). Instead of the void of nihilistic annihilation, it is the void of procreative life. For Johnson the Buddhist void is the ultimate symbol of ideology-free aesthetics—an endless supply of unpredictable and uncontained creativity that creates and destroys new forms, blending and modifying them as it creates. The ocean's procreative power works as a symbol on two levels: as a Zen Buddhist symbol and as the liberated and liberatory aesthetic that, for no particular reason other than the joy of creation, propagates new forms in a spirit of eternal playfulness.[7]

While Rutherford's second chapter in the log outlines a primarily Western worldview and briefly introduces readers to some of its limitations and paradoxes, the third chapter introduces readers to a contrasting Eastern perspective, a perspective that will have a profound impact on the crew and, most important, on Rutherford as he continues his process of development and aesthetic education. Rutherford's immersion in living history continues when he, the recently freed man of color, arrives to visit the slave-trading post in Bangalang, on the West coast of Africa, established by the Royal African Company in 1683, with a history of conflict between local natives and the Dutch, French, and English. In this setting, Rutherford is introduced to the Allmuseri as the tribe is being violently broken apart. Johnson details the core of slavery's brutality—its destructive fragmenting effect on the family and on individuals. Rutherford's witnessing of these and other incidents, such as women throwing babies overboard, turns his hair white, since he sees, unlike the white first mate, his own people being so cruelly subjugated.

The forced separations and violence they endure is particularly disorienting for the Allmuseri, who, as Rutherford learns, deeply embody an Eastern holism. They are a clan-state, "as close-knit as cells in the body" (*MP*, 58). In his notes for the novel, Johnson writes about the Allmuseri, "For the Allmuseri, every single human action, situation, and deed is the opportunity to practice sacrifice to their God, *was*, in fact, their God in action, each tribesman being but a transparency for his unfoldment; each deed to them, therefore, was shot full of spirituality . . . No object divorced from divinity. No person or thing for these Allmuseri could dwell outside the order of the Whole." Instead of stressing exploitative

---

7. Ross, *Three Ways*, 121; William Theodore de Bary, *The Buddhist Tradition*, 77–8.

individualism and self-reliance, the Allmuseri see in the republic, or larger state, an organic collectivity, interdependent, integrative, and interconnected. In his descriptions of them, Johnson employs the thinking of Zen Buddhism and its anti-individualism: "Each one of us is but a cell, as it were, in the body of the Great Self, a cell that comes into being, performs its functions, and passes away, transformed into another manifestation. Though we have temporary individuality, that temporary limited individuality is not either a true self or our true self. Our true self is the Great Self." Before being kidnapped by the slave traders, the Allmuseri seem to live a life of harmonious spirituality, liberated from constricting notions of selfhood and the destructive acquisitional thinking that Falcon's rule embodies, and, tragically, introduces them to.[8]

Middle Passage dramatizes the violent and tragic clash of radically different cultures. The cultural clash set in motion by the sequence of events has its ominous overtones—the crew draws straws to see who will catch a glimpse of the Allmuseri god, which is kept in the hold of the ship. Tommy O'Toole, the simultaneously fortunate and unfortunate cabin boy, is chosen, and he returns no longer sane, but blissfully altered. Through O'Toole's liberating experience in the hold of the ship, Johnson demonstrates the double-sidedness of spiritual liberation: how it separates the subject from him- or herself, perhaps permanently. Through Rutherford's artistic achievement, Johnson details O'Toole's out-of-body experience, in which he is immersed in another realm of consciousness, one more closely tied to the rhythms and mysteries of spiritual liberation than to realist narrative. O'Toole experiences a radically disorienting sense of wholeness in which he, the African God, and the song he finds himself singing become one: "and they were a single thing: singer, listener, and song, light spilling into light, the boundaries of inside and outside, here and there, today and tomorrow, obliterated as in the penetralia of the densest stars" (*MP*, 69). Through his encounter with the god, Tommy experiences a traumatic self-transcendence and an immediate and profound apprehension of a fundamental spiritual unity that revises individual identity and conventional categories of perception. As with Faith and Andrew's final liberations, Tommy has become a vehicle for divine aestheticism. In his merging with god and song, Tommy has become Emerson's transparent eyeball, or Wallace Steven's singer on the beach in "The Idea of Order at Key West," who "was the single artificer of the world . . . / And when she sang, the sea, / Whatever self it had, became the self."[9]

8. Charles Johnson, "The Writer's Notebook," 136; Ross, *Three Ways,* 145.
9. Wallace Stevens, *Modern Poems,* 97.

Such a change, witnessed and appreciated by Rutherford, causes him to be thought of as mad by the other crewmen, who fear being eaten by the god; they cannot appreciate his entrance into the voidness of another dimension. Since, however, *Middle Passage* was written for a more popular audience that would, presumably, have less patience for these kind of mystical flights than readers of *Oxherding Tale*, Tommy O'Toole is a minor character in the novel and does not occupy the central protagonist's role. Rutherford's appealingly sane character and narrative voice ground the narrative and provide its chronologically plotted continuity. Yet, Tommy's descent into the hold foreshadows Rutherford's own descent, which is less mysteriously described, and it allows Johnson to hint at the awesome power of nonrational, nondualistic Eastern mysticism, while still deploying the more accessible frame of the sea-adventure story.

In his recent article comparing Morrison's *Beloved* and *Middle Passage*, Vincent O'Keefe makes the compelling argument that Johnson's narrative techniques—including the single narrative voice—overly stress seriality or traditional plot linkages instead of the phenomenological principle of simultaneity—of seeing all perspectives at the same moment. He argues that Morrison's narrative techniques of "disorientation, incommensurability, and nonclosure help achieve the reader's sense of simultaneity" more effectively. O'Keefe's argument is very useful and well informed by phenomenological principle. While I agree that Johnson's use of Rutherford as a traditional narrator overly unifies the reader's experience of the novel and does not allow the reader to experience fully other modes of perception, such as Tommy O'Toole's in the ship's hold, Johnson's adherence to the "form" of the well-unified sea-adventure plot prevents him from emphasizing Morrison's modernist incommensurability. At the same time, Johnson's faithfulness to Buddhism's holism further prevents him from veering off into narrative fragmentation and nonclosure.[10]

However truncated, Rutherford's appreciation of Tommy's experience marks a new stage in his development, one in which he is moving away from the egoism defined by Falcon. On the plot level, however, he is still in the "middle," struggling to define his identity and establish his loyalties. Against his will, Rutherford has become Falcon's spy, reporting back to Falcon the crew's dissatisfactions and mutinous plans. He is also privy to the Allmuseri's plans to revolt. From this point on in the narrative, Rutherford (like Berkeley in "Menagerie: A Child's Fable") is caught

10. Vincent A. O'Keefe, "Reading Rigor Mortis: Offstage Violence and Excluded Middles in Johnson's *Middle Passage* and Morrison's *Beloved*," 644.

in the middle of complex and intersecting battles—crew against captain and Allmuseri against both crew and captain. He is both informer and mutineer. Like Andrew in *Oxherding Tale,* he finds himself in the midst of multiple battles, and he, like Andrew, must struggle to construct his own identity.

Culture and Aesthetics

Johnson's allegory about culture and philosophy operates right on the surface of the novel. As has been pointed out in much of the criticism about the novel, it's clear that the difference in cultures is philosophically based. Captain Falcon believes in the Cartesian dualism of mind and body; the Allmuseri take the opposing view. Given Johnson's Eastern bias, he, predictably, makes an implicit causal argument that Falcon's beliefs naturally lead to conflict, to oppression, to warfare. Johnson airs his philosophical views through Falcon, who states, after learning of the crew's plan to mutiny through Rutherford, that man, not the crew, is the problem. In an act of odd self-consciousness and self-reflection, Falcon is able to identify the root of man's problems, yet, at the same, time, continue to act in the same problematic way, blind to the wisdom of the Allumseri, whom he has so cruelly enslaved.

Johnson paints Cartesian dualism as a tragic philosophy, especially in its consequences for human history and human action. As Falcon says, the subject-object split is the "sign of a transcendental Fault, a deep crack in consciousness itself. Mind was made for murder" (*MP,* 98). Slavery, too, is the result of this deep "ontic wound" (*MP,* 98). As Johnson expresses in all of his work, this Western emphasis on conflict, on the split between selves, and on victory has had profoundly negative effects both on larger patterns of history (such as chattel-slavery) and on individual consciousness— a view taken to fantastic extremes when the pet shop self-destructively fractures in the denouement of "Menagerie: A Child's Fable." Part of the reason that the crew wants to mutiny is that they sense that Falcon has a death-wish—his philosophical perspective, in fact, leads to a longing for death and peace.

Johnson uses the elder Allmuseri Ngonyama to offer an alternative to Falcon's perspective. Like the Allmuseri God, Ngonyama embodies its core values. Instead of valuing warfare, victory, and the validation of an individual or group perspective, Ngonyama and the Allmuseri value life. They are dedicated to the principles of karma and the sacredness of life. In contrast to Western society's greed, the Allmuseri avoid fighting and stealing. They are able to heal themselves and do not eat meat.

Their language is incapable of abstractions and is expressed in stunningly beautiful pictograms, whose meanings preempt rational thought in favor of a single impressionistic experience. When Rutherford looks at the Allmuseri's picture language, he enters a pleasurably meditative, relaxed state, reflecting Johnson's own indebtedness to visual art as aesthetic stimulus for inspiration. Given their nonrationalistic language, the Allmuseri cannot grasp empirical science and are unable to do analysis or deconstruction, as Rutherford anachronistically points out.

As the differences in language suggest, the difference between Eastern and Western perspectives is primarily an aesthetic one. Where Falcon's only aesthetic sense is confined to the beauty of his weapons, the Allmuseri are living art, individual manifestations of spiritual beauty. Like the Swamp Woman, the Allmuseri are conjurers and magicians. Reminiscent of Reb's coffin making, Ngonyama employs a meditative technique when he carves a pig with astonishing technique. He carves magically, able to trace a pattern with his knife that efficiently and economically does its job, with no unaesthetic "hacking and rending" (*MP*, 76). Through Ngonyama, Johnson further explores and refines his conception of beauty and aestheticism—a definition that involves a Hemingwayesque purity of line, efficiency of motion, magic, and revelation.

In his portrait of Ngonyama's artistry, Johnson clearly draws again on a central Taoist parable from the collected writings of fourth-century B.C.E. Chinese Taoist Chuang-tzu. The parable concerns a cook's ox carving. When asked about his technique, the cook answers, "I follow the natural grain, letting knife find its way through the many hidden openings, taking advantage of what is there, never touching a ligament or tendon, much less a main joint . . . with a very slight movement of the knife, I cut the whole ox open. It falls apart like a clod of earth crumbling to the ground." At the end of the scriptural passage, his master, Lord Wen-hui exclaims, "Well done!" and adds, "From the words of my cook, I have learned the secret of growth." Similarly, through the gradual encroachment of Allmuseri Zen aesthetic spirituality into Rutherford's consciousness, he learns, as we will soon discuss, how to value life and to depart from the egoistic individualism that has characterized his identity at the beginning of the novel. It is through the act of writing about his experiences that Rutherford-as-artist learns the "secret of growth" and writes with the same grace of line and technique shown by the Toaist cook and Ngonyama. Johnson, however, does not fully pursue Rutherford's extraordinary mystical experiences near the end of his story because this would derail the fast-paced male-oriented plot that drives this sea-adventure story. Yet Rutherford's abbreviated reaction and experience with the Allmuseri god underscores the spiritual effect of exposure to this otherworldly aesthetic performance.[11]

Spirituality and Politics

When the ship is on its homeward journey, with various rebellions and mutinies being planned, Johnson slows the plot by providing more explanation of Rutherford's past and his relationship with his brother, Jackson, whom Rutherford has mentioned in passing several times earlier, always with contempt. Johnson uses the fifth chapter to explore the deepest aspects of Rutherford's consciousness—and his connection with an Allmuserian or Buddhist consciousness even before his journeys began—and the unresolved relationships he has with Jackson and his father, who died trying to escape when Rutherford was a boy.

Through Jackson, who resembles the Allmuseri so much he could "be one of their priests" (*MP*, 109), Johnson translates Eastern mysticism into the African American context, simultaneously emphasizing the particular and the universal. Brought up together on a plantation in southern Illinois, Rutherford and Jackson choose different strategies for revolt and subversion to counter their humiliating and dehumanizing status as bondsmen. Rutherford, in his life as a thief, gambler, and vandal, chooses the path of rebellion; Jackson chooses the path of slow-moving reform, of Allmuserian nonviolence, equivalent, in the American context, to the protest strategies of Dr. Martin Luther King Jr. Jackson matches every one of Rutherford's acts with an act of selflessness. Jackson is Rutherford's troubling alter-ego.

When confronted with the choice given to them by their dying owner, who asks them what they want done with all his property and possessions, Jackson, unlike Rutherford, decides to distribute the estate evenly among the slaves on the plantation and grant them their freedom. Although seen as obsequious by other slaves, Jackson is portrayed as an effective racial activist, able to overturn and subvert the racial power hierarchy with more potency than outright sedition by redefining and reshaping his role of manservant to further his own ends. Jackson's other-regarding, nonviolent, New Testament strategies of treating everyone the same, including worthy whites, confounds the definition of master-slave and eventually reverses the power structure, since, after his master's death Jackson "takes care" of his master's property by redistributing it among the workers. As Rutherford points out, Jackson's example and reversals undercut slavery's power hierarchy in an spiritually pure way. Jackson's

---

11. Feng and English, *Chuang Tsu*, 55.

nonviolent direct-action methods recall the activism of Dr. Martin Luther King Jr. and of Gandhi, both of whom incorporated spiritual principles, Eastern and Western, into their policies for social and racial reform, yet blended with the strategies of Johnson's satiric and subverting aesthetic which utilizes such techniques as juxtaposition and reversals.

In the depiction of the successful Allmuseri revolt and aftermath, Johnson makes his political biases clear, at least in terms of effective racial activism. In some ways an allegorical parody and corrective of the late sixties' Black Power movement and contemporary beliefs in Afrocentrism, the revolt pits the younger, more militant Allmuseri Diamelo against the elder, more moderate Ngonyama as leaders of the ship.

Diamelo, driven by his anger and hatred of his white tormentors, finds his identity and direction in the revolt, whereas Ngonyama, more traditional, seems incapacitated by his participation in the violence and its karmic results. Johnson's satiric parody of Diamelo's position is scathing and reminiscent of his scathing attacks on Black Nationalist leaders from his career as a political cartoonist. Rutherford depicts Diamelo's transition to political tribal leader as basically disingenuous and opportunistic. Through Rutherford's ironic tone, Johnson takes the position of the orthodox Allmuseri in criticizing Diamelo's ethnocentric and factionalized positions, since Diamelo is portrayed as overemphasizing the need to use only Allmuseri maps, eat only Allmuseri food, take only Allmuseri medicine, and avoid any usage of English.

Johnson undermines Diamelo's position in several other ways. He depicts Diamelo's solutions as ultimately unworkable and extremely unpopular among the remaining Allmuseri. He exposes Diamelo as paradoxically dependent on his oppressor's victimization of him. Diamelo suffers a loss when Falcon commits suicide since he depends on Falcon's existence for his identity. Diamelo, reminiscent of George Hawkins in *Oxherding Tale,* fixates on his victimization and is destroyed by it. Diamelo's position of victimology is dramatized as unstable in the depiction of his death—since his actions destroy all those in his path, including himself. When Rutherford emerges on deck, he steps over Diamelo's remains. No one in the line of fire of a late-firing cannon survives. When the cannon blows, it fills the deck with a deadly barrage of bricks and metal as if to echo the brick-throwing violence of the urban inner-city riots of the late sixties and early seventies. This apocalyptic result is reminiscent of the denouement of the short story "Menagerie: A Child's Fable," in which the conflicts between each interest group cause a massive conflagration. In this embedded politicized tableau in *Middle Passage,* Johnson repeats his warnings against militant racial separatism and brick-throwing violence as an effective means of combatting racial oppression since it results only in self-destruction.

This political allegory is neither as didactic as "Menagerie: A Child's Fable," nor as static as his cartoon attacks on Black Power leaders since Ngonyama's more moderate position does not triumph, as one might expect. Ngonyama, representing the wisdom of the elders, is incapacitated by his involvement in the violent assault on the crew due to its karmic penalties. His spirit is suddenly frozen in place by the enormity of the situation. He is disoriented, displaced, and empty after the violence. Ngonyama has become irrevocably lashed to Falcon's ship—his karmic purity and Eastern worldview forever poisoned by slavery, imprisonment, and forced exposure to Falcon's destructive, bifurcated Western Cartesianism, to the anti-aesthetic madness of dualism. Despite Johnson's obvious preferences, neither Diamelo's radicalism nor Ngonyama's more moderate strategies are able to withstand the ultimate destruction of their exposure to the toxic legacies of the West.

Epiphany

Before and after the violent Allmuseri revolt, Rutherford moves through a familiar pattern of development as he, like his predecessors Andrew and Faith, battles to define his identity. After throwing the rotting and disintegrating body of a dead Allmuseri overboard, an Allmuseri who resembles Rutherford, he faces a similar psychological disintegration. It is not until he confronts the deepest, most unresolved parts of himself and his past that Rutherford is able to overcome his despair. Like Andrew, Rutherford must come to terms with the haunting memories of his long-dead father, who was killed in an escape attempt when Rutherford was a small child. After his death, Riley becomes for Rutherford a troubling and haunting presence, forever the fixed object of guilty recollections and desires for reconciliation.

Via the Allmuseri god, Rutherford achieves a cathartic epiphany. In the transparent, massive god image, Rutherford sees—in similar fashion to what Andrew sees in the Soulcatcher's fluid tattoo tapestry—a comprehensive history of his life, including his father's life and murder. In this filmic "seriality of images," he hears his father's death cry and his father's breath, which, poetically, join with the voices and breaths of thousands of others, what Rutherford calls "a mosaic of voices within voices" (*MP*, 171). In this complex passage, Johnson explores the sudden expansion of perception and includes one of the novel's central Buddhist images which recalls the Zen conception of the void. His father's image is conjoined with a larger mystical whole, "as waves vanish into water" (*MP*, 171), which teaches Rutherford to distrust the artificiality, or the fiction, of black identity (or any racial identity) and to accept a more Eastern notion of identity, or nonidentity. His father's presence, momentarily gone, returns to him in a collective vision of reassuring collectivism embodied in a larger We. In this transcendent aural and visual experience, Rutherford hears in this mosaic the origins of his self and his father's. Just as his father is absorbed into the larger whole, like a drop of water into the ocean, Rutherford too recognizes his newfound and liberating connection to others, living and dead. Rutherford has resolved the pain of his father's memory by incorporating his father into himself, just as Andrew, in *Oxherding Tale*, became "my father's father, and he my child" (*OT*, 176) in his reconciliation experience. In place of Western beliefs in a separate identity and self, Rutherford accepts an alternate vision offered through his interaction with this ancient African god. Because of this experience Rutherford no longer will feel orphaned. No longer will he fear, as he did earlier, the ocean's annihilating effect on human personality, since he has revised his notions of selfhood and identity to embrace fluidity and change. Although the intensity of the experience causes Rutherford to faint, he awakens deeply changed.

Rutherford's Synthetic Empowerment

In emphasizing Rutherford's transfiguring writing, Johnson is repeating one of the primary conventions of the slave narrative. As Houston Baker points out, "Only by grasping the word could he [the slave] engage in the speech acts that would ultimately define his selfhood. Further, the slave's task was primarily of creating a human and liberated self rather than of projecting one that reflected a particular landscape or tradition. His problem was not to answer Crevecoeur's question, 'What then is the American, this new man?' It was, rather, the problem of being itself." Certainly, the "quest for being" found in the genre-defining autobiographical narratives of Frederick Douglass, Harriet Jacobs, and Booker T. Washington are well known. But it is through the process of writing that this quest is resolved and verified. Johnson's adaptation of this movement toward selfhood and freedom incorporates and revises the slave narrative's conventional narrative arc by, paradoxically, modifying Western ideals of selfhood through the interjection of Eastern thinking about individual and communal identity.[12]

12. Houston Baker Jr., "Autobiographical Acts," 245.

In these revelatory writing sessions, Rutherford admits to being "a wreck of the *Republic*" (*MP*, 190). He realizes that instead of an individual self, he is a mosaic compilation of influences. His confrontation with Falcon and the Allmuseri has created in him a sense of indebtedness that he had heretofore never felt. Like the Allmuseri, whose every action bespeaks history and ritual, so much so that it "virtually rendered the individual performer invisible" (*MP*, 166), Rutherford's "self" is now an integrative mosaic self; "Rutherford" is indistinguishable from his influences "as ocean and wave" (*MP*, 166). As an artist figure, Rutherford has learned, in typical Zen Buddhist fashion, to erase himself from the center of the narrative and to stress instead the broader currents of communal and historical identity, interfused with the rhythms and images of nature. In this case Rutherford's writing moves from a focus on his own desires to how he can help others, specifically the three orphaned Allmuseri children who miraculously survived the shipwreck.

In helping others Rutherford "writes" a happy ending, using the strengths from his integrative or additive identity. Rutherford is able to synthesize what he has been and what he has learned to defeat the Papa Zeringue, the New Orleans gangster who is a rival suitor for Isadora. Rutherford uses the Brazilian fighting technique *capoeira*, which the Allmuseri used to defeat the ship's crew, to best Santos, Papa's mammoth bodyguard. He also blackmails Papa Zeringue who, as Falcon earlier revealed, was one of the three investors in the *Republic*, by threatening to expose his scandalous connection with the slave trade. These strategies learned from his life as a con man and thief are put to good use, since he forces Papa into agreeing to support financially the surviving orphans, leading the surprised and pleased Isadora to marvel at the changes in Rutherford. *Middle Passage*, like *Oxherding Tale*, is a drama of domestic inclusion that centers around the powers of the family to rebuild and to provide the foundations for individual and communal contentment.

Johnson parallels Rutherford's development in the characterization of Josiah Squibb, the ship's cook. Squibb begins the narrative a caricature of the drunken sailor, complete with a sarcastic, wisecracking parrot. In his lifelong search for the perfect woman, Squibb, like Kujichagulia and Barrett, is obsessed with perfection and finding the one truth or answer. To find contentment, Squibb had to lose everything, face death, and revise his perceptions. Unlike Johnson's previous minor characters afflicted with the same motivations, Squibb undergoes a compelling change which parallels Rutherford's own. At the end of the novel he serves the ship in whatever capacity he is needed, as cook, surgeon, and helmsmen. Through concentrating only on his everyday work, Squibb has found a significant Zen or Taoist path for achieving contentment and for moving beyond the schisms that Falcon identified as plaguing man's existence.

Just as Squibb's outlook has shifted from one predominately wedded to a destructive Cartesianism and Platonism to Zen Buddhist emphasis on the here and now, Rutherford experiences this shift in perspective as a result of his exposure to the Zen Buddhist perspectives of the Allmuseri. At the end of the narrative Rutherford is no longer enthralled by romantic visions of adventure. Instead, he has adopted a new, slightly paradoxical way of viewing the world. He confesses that now each person possesses such a profound uniqueness that Rutherford is unable to generalize about them apart from their actions. Rutherford's Zen-seeing includes giving primacy to individual experience and avoiding fixed platonic universals that run the risk of taking away the responsibility of creating perception from the individual perceiver. The nominalistic Zen seer is "being pushed relentlessly toward personal *experience,* toward an illuminating *realization* of the unity of all life, the Is-ness or Such-ness of existence itself." At the end of the narrative, Rutherford learns to appreciate and to live in the present. Through the unexpected vehicle of Eastern philosophy, Rutherford has learned a profoundly precise analytic technique.[13]

This development points, however, to yet another apparent contradiction in Johnson's aesthetic. On the one hand Johnson has shown Rutherford moving in the narrative toward a mystical appreciation for the connectedness of all life and all forms; on the other hand, he has learned, through Zen, that everything contains its own radical uniqueness or distinctiveness. Perhaps one of the reasons for Zen's popularity in the West is its similarity with the scientific method of analysis, something Johnson hints at in an interview in *African American Review*: "Early Buddhism, by the way, has often been called a very rudimentary form of phenomenology—the two have much in common in respect to their forms of 'radical empiricism.'" Yet for Zen Buddhists the intensely analytic method of observation leads, somewhat illogically, to a release from thought, to a rejection of distinctions between "this" and "that." Radical empiricism relies essentially on analytic separation, inference, and extrapolation. For the empiricist, this analytic process leads to a clarified scientific methodology—a celebration of the very rational, word-bound mind that Buddhism rejects as the ultimate phase of enlightenment or liberation. Johnson may be using these tensions between the analytic and the mystical to fuel his integrative technique—to see what happens when they are put

13. Ross, *Three Ways,* 155.

together to form something new, yet the apparent contradictions that exist in Zen also exist in Johnson's writing in ways that are not as apparent in romantic thinking.[14]

Despite these contradictions, *Middle Passage* argues powerfully for the rewards of the cosmopolitan spiritual imagination—for telling each other our secrets across racial and national barriers and for recognizing our commonalities instead of our differences. For instance, Rutherford can see Squibb's transformative empowerment. In him Rutherford feels the "perfectly balanced crosscurrents of culture in him" (*MP*, 176) that Squibb uses to overcome problems. Through Rutherford and Squibb's character development, Johnson shows how enriching immersion into the global relations can be. Rutherford enters into the intersubjective "inescapable network of mutuality" that King envisioned and thereby emerging more complete and content.

Conclusions

In his final plans to marry Isadora, return to the Midwest to become a farmer, live near his saintly brother Jackson, and adopt Baleka, one of the orphaned Allmuseri children, Rutherford has completed one stage of his philosophical, spiritual, and psychological development. He, like Andrew from *Oxherding Tale*, finds his peace and contentment, his Way or *dharma*, in his duties as a householder and father. Where in earlier stages of his development Rutherford was concerned only with accumulating excessive experience as a thief, playboy, or writer-artist, now he is devoted to serving others and living responsibly.

As in *Faith and the Good Thing*, where Faith's sexual union with Alpha Omega Holmes melts them together, overcoming divisions of gender, in Rutherford's final position in *Middle Passage* he attains a spiritual union with Isadora that overcomes the sexist preconceptions that earlier stereotyped his view of women. As they lie together in the closing pages of the novel, Rutherford and Isadora reject desire in favor of something else more permanent. Rutherford ends longing for the transcendent union that Faith is able to achieve with Holmes. Like Andrew and Peggy, Rutherford and Isadora look forward to the future together, when, perhaps, they can achieve that romantic union. For now, they must accept their situation. The novel's final sentence, which pictures them drifting to sleep in each others' arms, emphasizes the "countless seas of suffering" (*MP*, 209) that they must yet endure as a couple.

14. Michael Boccia, "An Interview with Charles Johnson," 616.

The final sentence indicates that, despite his progress, Rutherford's quest for harmonious being is still not complete. He has not achieved *moksha* or spiritual release or liberation. Uncharacteristically somber, the novel's final sentence revises Rutherford's previously comic tone, indicating that he has profoundly changed as writer and character and has, perhaps, begun the process of following the Buddhist eight-fold path of enlightenment, since the first of the four holy truths is the recognition of suffering. In this uncharacteristically modest ending, also, Johnson may be seeking to show the movement toward a more rigorous Zen self-abnegation; the self-effacing tone matches Rutherford's remarkable transformation from romantic hero and artist figure to a character with extremely modest aspirations more suited to the self-effacing and private spiritual seeker. As the ending of *Middle Passage* shows, Johnson has yet to create an artistic figure who develops his or her selflessness—artistry and spirituality seem to be mutually exclusive in Johnson's fiction. Instead, perhaps aware of the difficulties of pursuing such a character, Johnson ends his narratives with the initial steps toward the self-emptying processes that precede Eastern spiritual progress.

The State Revised

Unlike in his previous novels, Johnson makes the application and relevance of his thinking explicitly political, at least in regards to the responsibilities and characteristics of citizenship. Rutherford's revised mode of perception affects his view of America, and he longs to return, in spite of its legacy of racism and his history as a slave. He professes his allegiance to this complex "cauldron of mongrels" (*MP*, 179). Rutherford's synthetic empowerment has rendered him somewhat more prepared to deal with the day-to-day oppression and discrimination against people of color in the American republic. Perhaps because of his own emptying out of a Western conception of "self," Rutherford now feels settled in and indebted to a country that is itself in a state of constant change and flux, despite its slaveholding practices.

While conservative critics such as George Will have been quick to embrace the novel's patriotic message, *Middle Passage* in no way supports a nationalistic or even a conservative message. Through Falcon's character, Johnson parodies neoconservatives such as Allan Bloom and Dinesh D'Souza, whose pessimistic commentaries on American culture warn against the impending breakdown of American society due to the promotion of multiculturalism and the demands of special interest groups. In a scene reminiscent of Bloom's *The Closing of the American Mind,*

Falcon tells Rutherford of a dream he had in which he foresaw the complete breakdown of American culture, similar to Bloom's bleak visions of an undereducated America. Johnson distances himself from the neoconservative pundits by satirizing their paranoia and showing that, indeed, America is already a nonhierarchical complex merger and synthesis of nationalities. In one scene, passengers aboard the *Juno* sing "Have You Ever Been in New Orleans?" and provide evidence of Johnson's view. The song's lyrics depict a nation that replicates the wicked diversity that Johnson champions in *Being and Race* as one of his aesthetic ideals. The song celebrates interracial marriage and the dizzying range of human experience included in the country, which is "a nation of a queer place," and "a progeny of all colors" (*MP*, 189). As this song and the novel illustrate, America includes a kaleidoscopic of races, nationalities, and behavior, indicative of Johnson's espousal of the integrative state's ambiguous diversity, uncontained by any single perspective.

Middle Passage and *Invisible Man*

In its conclusions and implications, *Middle Passage* is more closely allied with Ralph Ellison's *Invisible Man* than with any other literary precedent, although there are significant differences. In their belief in integration, Ellison and Johnson share similar animating ideological visions, thus their novels share similar conclusions about democracy and interracial relations.

Just as Rutherford recognizes his interrelatedness to everyone and everything else in the republic, Invisible Man realizes the diversity inherent in the United States. Echoing the rhetoric of democratic ideals, Invisible Man states, "America is woven of many strands; I would recognize them and let it so remain . . . Our fate is to become one, and yet many—This is not prophecy, but description." As the result of his process of education, Invisible Man has become more comfortable with ambiguity and life's "absurd diversity": "Now I know men are different and that all life is divided and that only in division is there true health." Although stressing Western divisiveness instead of holism, *Invisible Man* shares a concern with demonstrating the multiplicity, heterogeneity, and ambiguity of life in America.[15]

Where Johnson uses the vehicle of Buddhism in *Middle Passage* to transcend dualism and divisiveness and to champion his beliefs in a kind of spiritual integrationism, Ellison uses African American jazz; these similar yet

15. Ralph Ellison, *Invisible Man*, 563–4.

different metaphors illuminate the two authors' differences as well. Like Louis Armstrong, Invisible Man has made an art of being invisible. In his state of nascent hibernation, he plays "the invisible music of his isolation," that allows him the freedom to "slip into the breaks and look around," offering him an expanded mode of perception. Invisible Man slips out of chronological, linear time to interrogate America's tendencies toward conformity and group-think. Music, or the imagination, has the power to transcend word-bound ideology and conformist ideologies, whether the brotherhood's socialism or Ras's black nationalism. At the funeral of Todd Clifton, another character who has slipped out of time, Invisible Man reflects on the power of music: "It was not the words, for they were all the same old slave-borne words; it was as though he'd changed the emotion beneath the words while yet the old longing, resigned, transcendent emotion still sounded above, now deepened by that something for which the theory of Brotherhood had given no name." In this pivotal scene, Invisible Man's perception is profoundly altered. He looks into the Harlem crowd, and, for the first time, he sees specific individuals. He is disabused of the socialist ideology that had ruled his thinking, realizing that the African American community contains distinct individuals more complex and ambiguous than one unifying theory of identity and history can account for. Like Rutherford's particularistic "Zen-seeing," Invisible Man learns to distrust theories that fix experience into convenient categories, such as "good," or "evil." Freed from conformist ideologies, Invisible Man is empowered to examine each event and each person as a complex intersection of often conflicting influences. Part of his invisibility is caused by the fact that he has tried to erase the overbearing influence of others to construct an individualized vision, however incomplete at the novel's resolution.[16]

Like Rutherford, Invisible Man's sense of self is constantly changing as he moves forward to reconcile those parts of his past he has previously tried to suppress. While attending Clifton's funeral, Invisible Man thinks, "And now all past humiliations became precious parts of my experience, and for the first time, leaning against that stone wall in the sweltering night, I began to accept my past and, as I accepted it, I felt memories welling up within me. . . . They were me; they defined me. I was my experiences and my experiences were me." With "all boundaries down," Invisible Man can now see more completely. At the end of the novel, Invisible Man waits, anticipating the next conflicting stage of his identity formation. Invisible Man likens his act of artistic self-fashioning and self-creation to playing

16. Ibid., 13, 8, 442.

music; by the end of the narrative he has become an enactment of the liberating yet conflicted synthesis inherent in jazz.[17]

Ellison's belief in the transcendent power of jazz or of art as a pathway to moments of "high consciousness" is a complex one, not untouched by contradictions, since there is a "cruel contradiction implicit in the art form itself. For true jazz is an art of individual assertion within and against the group." The individual musician defines and loses identity at the same moment since there is a simultaneous assertion of individual identity and immersion into the "collectivity" of jazz forms and tradition.[18]

Johnson's Buddhist holism in *Middle Passage* would have it differently. While still stressing the integration and synthesis of identity, as in Rutherford's epiphanic moment with the Allmuseri god or Andrew's epiphany at the end of *Oxherding Tale,* Johnson resolves Ellison's modernist paradox of alienation, competition, and interdependence (of losing identity even when finding it) by interrogating the notion of a separate identity. Johnson, deeply influenced by Buddhist doctrine that denies the presence of a permanent, substantial, independent, and metaphysical self, is more comfortable with the mystical and phenomenological polymorphy of the self than Ellison seems to be. Invisible Man hopes to construct a new, more satisfying identity that would replace his invisibility and formlessness and seems threatened by pure imaginative play, or the possibilities of forever changing shape in the way that Faith does at the end of her novel. For instance, Invisible Man relates, "A beautiful girl once told me of a recurring nightmare in which she lay in the center of a large dark room and felt her face expand until it filled the whole room, becoming a formless mass while her eyes ran in bilious jelly up the chimney. And so it is with me. Without light I am not only invisible, but formless as well; and to be unaware of one's form is to live a death." Johnson replaces the terrifying Western metaphor of "bilious jelly" and formlessness with the metaphor of the life-affirming Buddhist void, into which individual identity is comfortingly subsumed into the whole, "as waves vanish into the water" (*MP,* 171).[19]

Despite this difference—which revolves around the issue of spirituality —both artists use their novelistic reflections on identity to limn the responsibilities of citizenship. In *his* National Book Award acceptance speech in 1953, Ellison asserts that the "chief significance" of *Invisible Man* is in its "experimental attitude, and its attempt to return to the mood of

17. Ibid., 496.
18. Ralph Ellison, *Shadow and Act,* 234.
19. Ellison, *Invisible Man,* 6–7.

personal moral responsibility for democracy which typified the best of our nineteenth-century fiction." Instead of taking them away from the political realm, or creating a reclusive aesthetic diffidence, both artists work to craft literature that emphasizes a democratic Republic. Their novels construct the philosophical foundations that support the politics of integrationism: a system that recognizes King's "network of mutuality" and interracial cooperation. *Invisible Man's* final status of alienation and exile, however, emphasizes the problematics of African American citizenship in America in the fifties more vividly than Johnson's current rendition.[20]

In comparison to *Invisible Man, Middle Passage* too quickly resolves the fascinating issues about the relationship of self to state that it introduces. Rutherford's development from rogue to responsible citizen, preaching patriotism and the need for devotion to everyone in the Republic, seems imposed from without in the final chapter as Johnson forces the social and spiritual implications of his character's evolution. Especially as it relates to his wider community in slaveholding America, Rutherford's growth seems abstractly idea rather than character driven. In contrast, the portrait of Invisible Man's complex fall from innocence is a powerful and haunting meditation on the concomitant difficulties and possibilities of interdependence and integrative national community.

Johnson owes much to Ellison's artistic achievement and his aesthetics. More exciting, perhaps, than parallels between *Invisible Man* and *Middle Passage* is the promise of Johnson's achievement to come, as he continues to bring his invigorating and eclectic literary vision to bear on issues of long-lasting and topical importance. If we are to accept Ellison's modernist assertion that through novels and art "we anticipate the resolution of those world problems of humanity which for a moment seem to those who are in awe of statistics completely insoluble," then we anticipate *Dreamer's* impact on a racial climate much more polarized and violent than the one that received *Invisible Man* in 1947.[21]

20. Ellison, *Shadow and Act,* 102.
21. Ibid., 106.

Conclusion

Beyond Race through
Spirituality

As the momentum of Johnson's development suggests, Johnson is moving toward a raceless vision of America, and of human community in general. The transcendence of race occurs often in the idealized *denouements* of his novels, as with Faith's form-switching or with Rutherford's espousal of a mosaic, additive identity. Although Johnson has taken us to the gate of a new vision of a ethnic identity or non-identity, he has not fully crossed that gate's threshold to explore in depth what such a community or individual would look like.

In the very short story, "The Work of the World" (1994), Johnson takes the next step of his evolving integrative aesthetic to further revise contemporary discussions of race and politics. In a response to Peter Blume's surrealist painting, "The Rock" (1948), Johnson wrote this fictional meditation on identity and community—another example of Johnson's reliance on visual art for inspiration. Blume's surrealist painting depicts a post-apocalyptic landscape that has been devastated by war. The figures in the painting are shown working to rebuild their world by shoveling, hammering, moving wood, stones, and concrete. In the middle of the painting stands a huge circular rock, jaggedly split in half—a chilling symbol of the destroyed planet.

The story takes place in the breathless moment just after the Hindu God Shiva's act of destruction and just before his act of creation. The characters exist in a kind of negative space, outside the realm of linear time. As they work together to rebuild their community they are virtually indistinguishable from one another, known only by the jobs they perform. The resentments and divisions that caused the world's destruction have disintegrated in the survivalistic aftermath. Johnson projects his vision of a fully spiritualized community dedicated to cooperative, selfless values into a utopian futuristic realm.

As in much of Johnson's fiction, the Western notion of the "self" is replaced in this story by a more aesthetically beautiful image—the luminous moment at which the self is absorbed into the larger mystical whole. At the end of the story the narrator stares meditatively into the fire, watching the sparks rise up, flare, and then disappear into the night. This particular image recurs throughout his fiction, with Andrew, for example, watching the sparking fire before moving into the white world. The central character in "The Work of the World" asks the great existential question if this one moment of individual life and death is worth all the suffering and struggle of human existence. The narrator answers affirmatively with the closing statement, "An instant might as well be centuries." In other words, Johnson implies, if you see time as nonlinear and cyclical (as do Hindus), the Western fear of impermanence is molified. Further, if you see the ephemeral rising up and fading away of individual existence as an aesthetic moment, the threat is turned into a blessing. The kwoon, or spiritual community depicted in "The Work of the World," shows Johnson taking the next step in his aesthetic evolution as he envisions communal life-artistry dedicated to creating a society with a strong foundation of moral values and Eastern selflessness.[1]

The direction of Johnson's politics and aesthetics seems clear. "The Work of the World" contains the logical endpoint of Johnson's evolving aesthetic as it intensifies its claims of social and moral relevance. Using religious traditions from around the world, especially those emanating from the East, Johnson argues for the benefits of social duty for individuals and for a harmonious and cooperative society. Essentially a Romantic, who shows the limitations of the ideal of the ego-centered Romantic hero, Johnson reincarnates liberal humanism, integrationism, and inward-turning spirituality as time-honored and still valid ways to overcome the divisions between people. That no such Gandhiesque or Kingesque community actually exists does not seem to dampen Johnson's spirits along these lines. The current ethnic and religious violence in Sri Lanka between the Buddhists and the Hindus is a particularly striking example of the gap between Eastern non-violent spiritual doctrine and political reality. Because of its links with the prophetic power of the imagination, fiction, for Johnson, seems to stand apart from reality. Its "good" is defined by its ability to imagine something else, something better yet to occur in

1. Charles Johnson, "The Work of the World," 100.

the future. In the words of another Romantic moralist, Fitzgerald's Nick Carraway, "tomorrow we will run faster, stretch out our arms farther . . . And one fine morning."[2]

In a contemporary academic context forged in a difficult time of government underfunding, attacks on higher education, and increasingly urgent appeals for equity, the focus, for literary critics and African American authors alike, has largely been on redressing the wrongs of the past in the the present rather than on envisioning a harmonious and collaborative future, which was more a part of the cold war liberal agenda. Johnson as spiritualized liberal humanist set in this context seems purposefully and provocatively antiquated as he looks forward and backward at the same moment. As his exposure continues to grow, it will be fascinating to watch the critical debates which will cluster around his diverse productions in cartooning, film, criticism, and fiction, which, despite the artistic genre, are all animated by a similar integrative spiritual aesthetic.

One hopes that "The Work and the World" will not be the final word in Johnson's evolving aesthetic vision. Important to an artist as fundamentally idealistic and spiritually oriented as Johnson will be the harsh glare of self-reflexive skepticism to counteract, at times, the golden glow of spiritual immanence. His fiction can achieve added resonance if he addresses such questions as: Is it possible or even desirable to live without divisions along ethnic, economic, and gender lines? Is art always a dreamy, apolitical fantasy? Is apoliticism a political statement by encouraging quiescence and indirectly affirming the status quo? Is promoting King's integrationism in today's context an act of social responsibility or a sophisticated means of avoidance? How can Eastern philosophy be translated into the American social context in a politically meaningful way that will improve people's lives? Such self-scrutinizing explorations will allow Johnson to avoid the dangers of predictability and to provide a valuable intellectual and artistic service for the dawning twenty-first century.

2. F. Scott Fitzgerald, *The Great Gatsby*, 189.

<h1 style="text-align:center">Bibliography</h1>

Arnold, Matthew. *The Portable Matthew Arnold,* edited by Lionel Trilling. New York: Viking Press, 1960.

Awkward, Michael. *Inspiriting Influences.* New York: Columbia University Press, 1989.

Baker, Houston, Jr. *Blues, Ideology and Afro-American Literature.* Chicago: University of Chicago Press, 1984.

———. "Autobiographical Acts and the Voice of the Southern Slave." In *The Slave's Narrative,* edited by Charles T. Davis and Henry Louis Gates, Jr., 242–61. New York: Oxford University Press, 1985.

Baraka, Amiri. *Home.* New York: Morrow, 1966.

———. "Why I Changed My Ideology: Black Nationalism and Social Revolution." *Black World* 9 (July 1975): 30–42.

Beardsley, Monroe C. *Aesthetics from Classical Greece to the Present.* New York: Macmillan, 1966.

Blue, Marian. "An Interview with Charles Johnson." *AWP Chronicle* 25 (February 1993): 1–8.

Boccia, Michael. "An Interview with Charles Johnson." *African American Review* 30 (winter 1996): 611–18.

Bracey, John H., Jr., August Meier, and Elliot Rudwick, eds. Introduction to *Black Nationalism in America.* New York: Bobbs-Merrill, 1970.

Burns, W. Haywood. "The Black Muslims in America: A Reinterpretation." In *Black Liberation Politics,* edited by Edward Greer, 72–85. Boston: Allyn & Bacon, 1971.

Byrd, Rudolph P. "*Oxherding Tale* and *Siddhartha*: Philosophy, Fiction, and the Emergence of a Hidden Tradition." *African American Review* 30.4 (winter 1996): 549–58.

Byrom, Thomas. *Dhammapada.* Boston: Shambhala, 1993.

Coleridge, Samuel Taylor. *Biographia Literaria.* London: Oxford University Press, 1907.

Conze, Edward. *Buddhist Scriptures*. New York: Penguin Books, 1959.

Dardess, George. "Bringing Comic Books to Class." *College English* 57.2 (February 1995): 213–22.

Davis, Arthur P., and Sterling Brown, eds. *The Negro Caravan*. New York: Arno Press, 1969.

de Bary, William Theodore, ed. *The Buddhist Tradition*. New York: Vintage Books, 1969.

Deutsch, Eliot, ed. *The Bhagavad Gita*. New York: Holt, Rinehart & Winston, 1968.

Dixon, Melvin. "Singing Swords: The Literary Legacy of Slavery." In *The Slave's Narrative,* edited by Charles T. Davis and Henry Louis Gates, Jr., 298–317. New York: Oxford University Press, 1985.

Dubey, Madhu. *Black Women Novelists and the Nationalist Aesthetic*. Bloomington: Indiana University Press, 1994.

Du Bois, W. E. B. *The Souls of Black Folk*. Cutchogue, N. Y.: Buccaneer Books, 1976.

Ellison, Ralph. Introduction to *Invisible Man*. New York: Vintage International, 1995.

———. *Invisible Man*. New York: Vintage Books, 1972.

———. *Shadow and Act*. New York: Random House, 1953.

Feng, Gia-Fu, and Jane English, eds. *Chuang Tsu: The Inner Chapters*. New York: Random House, 1974.

Fitzgerald, F. Scott. *The Great Gatsby*. New York: Macmillan, 1992.

Gardner, John. *The Art of Fiction*. New York: Random House, 1983.

———. *On Moral Fiction*. New York: Basic Books, 1977.

———. *On Writers and Writing*. Reading, Mass.: Addison-Wesley, 1994.

Gates, Henry Louis, Jr. *Figures in Black*. New York: Oxford University Press, 1987.

———. *The Signifying Monkey*. New York: Oxford University Press, 1988.

Gleason, William. "The Liberation of Perception: Charles Johnson's *Oxherding Tale*." *Black American Literature Forum* 25 (winter 1991): 705–28.

Graham, A. C. *Chuang-tzu*. London: George Allen & Unwin, 1981.

Harper, Phillip Brian. "Nationalism and Social Division in Black Arts Poetry of the 1960s." *Critical Inquiry* 19 (winter 1993): 234–55.

Harvey, Peter. *An Introduction to Buddhism*. Cambridge: Cambridge University Press, 1990.

Heidegger, Martin. "The Origin of the Work of Art." In *Martin Heidegger: Basic Writings,* edited by David Farrell Krell, 144–87. New York: Harper & Row, 1977.

Hesse, Hermann. *Siddhartha*. New York: Bantam Books, 1971.

Hixon, Lex. *Coming Home*. Burdett, N. Y.: Larson Publications, 1989.

Ihde, Don. *Existential Technics*. Albany: State University of New York Press, 1983.

Johnson, Charles. "Absence of Black Middle-Class Images Has Global Impact." *National Minority Politics* 4 (November 1993): 7, 22.

———. *Being and Race*. Bloomington: Indiana University Press, 1988.

———. *Black Humor*. Chicago: Johnson Publishing, 1970.

———. "Charles Johnson." Vol. 18, *Contemporary Authors Autobiography Series*, edited by Joyce Nakamura. Detroit: Gale Research, 1994.

———. "The Color Black." *New York Times Book Review*, 23 May 1993, 16.

———. "Consolation." *Callaloo* 4 (October 1978): 95–105.

———. "Creating the Political Cartoon." *Scholastic Editor* (February 1973): 8–13.

———. *Faith and the Good Thing*. New York: Viking Press, 1974.

———. "The Gift of the *Osuo*." *African American Review* 30 (December 1996): 519–26.

———. "The Green Belt: A Play for Television." *African American Review* 30 (December 1996): 559–78.

———. *Half-Past Nation Time*. California: Aware Press, 1972.

———. Introduction to *On Writers and Writing*. Reading, Mass.: Addison-Wesley, 1994.

———. Introduction to *Oxherding Tale*. New York: Plume, 1995.

———. "Inventing Africa." *New York Times Book Review*, 21 June 1992, 8.

———. "John Gardner as Mentor." *African American Review* 30 (winter 1996): 619–24.

———. "Journal Entries on the Death of John Gardner." *New Myths* 9 (fall 1992): 269–76.

———. "The King We Left Behind." *Common Quest* 1, no. 2 (fall 1996): 7–10.

———. "Kwoon." In *Prize Stories 1993. The O'Henry Awards*, edited by William Abrahams, 325–38. New York: Doubleday, 1993.

———. "Letters to John Gardner, 1974–1976," edited by Jessica Harris. Unpublished.

———. *Middle Passage*. New York: Macmillan, 1990.

———. "National Book Award Acceptance Speech." *TriQuarterly* 82 (fall 1991): 208–9.

———. *Oxherding Tale*. Bloomington: Indiana University Press, 1982.

———. "A Phenomenology of *On Moral Fiction*." In *Thor's Hammer: Essays on John Gardner*, edited by Jeff Henderson, 147–56. Conway: University of Central Arkansas Press, 1985.

————. "A Phenomenology of the Black Body." *Michigan Quarterly Review* 32 (fall 1993): 590–605.

————. "The Philosopher and the American Novel." In *In Search of a Voice*. Washington, D. C.: Library of Congress, 1991.

————. "Philosophy and Black Fiction." *Obsidian* 6, nos. 1–2 (1980): 55–61.

————. "Searching for the Dreamer." *Seattle Times,* 14 January 1996, B5.

————. "The Singular Vision of Ralph Ellison." *Washington Post,* 20 April 1994, C1, C4.

————. *The Sorcerer's Apprentice.* New York: Plume Books, 1994.

————. "Where Fiction and Philosophy Meet." *American Visions* 3 (June 1988): 36, 47–8.

————. "Whole Sight: Notes on New Black Fiction." *Callaloo* 7 (fall 1984): 1–6.

————. "The Work of the World." In *Transforming Vision,* edited by Edward Hirsch, 100. Chicago: Art Institute of Chicago and Bulfinch Press, 1994.

————. "The Writer's Notebook." *Zyzzyva* 8 (fall 1992): 124–42.

Karegna, Ron. "Black Cultural Nationalism." In *The Black Aesthetic,* edited by Addison Gayle, Jr., 32–8. Garden City, N. Y.: Doubleday & Company, 1971.

King, Coretta Scott. *The Words of Martin Luther King, Jr.* New York: Newmarket Press, 1987.

Kinsley, David R. *Hinduism: A Cultural Perspective.* Englewood Cliffs, N. J.: Prentice Hall, 1993.

Levine, George. "Introduction: Reclaiming the Aesthetic." In *Aesthetics and Ideology,* edited by George Levine, 1–28. New Brunswick, N. J.: Rutgers University Press, 1994.

Little, Jonathan. "Charles Johnson's Revolutionary *Oxherding Tale.*" *Studies in American Fiction* 19 (autumn 1991): 141–51.

————. "An Interview with Charles Johnson." *Contemporary Literature* 34 (summer 1993): 159–81.

McCartney, John T. *Black Power Ideologies.* Philadelphia: Temple University Press, 1992.

McCullough, Ken. "Reflections on Film, Philosophy, and Fiction: An Interview with Charles Johnson." *Callaloo* 4 (October 4, 1978): 118–28.

Morrison, Toni. *Beloved.* New York: New American Library, 1987.

————. "Rootedness: The Ancestor as Foundation." In *Black Women Writers,* edited by Mari Evans, 339–45. New York: Doubleday, Anchor Press, 1983.

Nash, William R. "Two Views of Desire: Charles Johnson's *Faith and the Good Thing*, Dreiser's *Sister Carrie*, and the Idea of Antinaturalism." Paper presented at the Modern Language Association Convention, Washington, D. C., December 1996.

Neal, Larry. "The Black Arts Movement." In *The Black Aesthetic*, edited by Addison Gayle, Jr., 272–90. Garden City, N. Y.: Doubleday & Company, 1971.

———. "Some Reflections on the Black Aesthetic." In *The Black Aesthetic*, edited by Addison Gayle, Jr., 13–26. Garden City, N. Y.: Doubleday & Company, 1971.

O'Keefe, Vincent A. "Reading Rigor Mortis: Offstage Violence and Excluded Middles in Johnson's *Middle Passage* and Morrison's *Beloved*." *African American Review* 30 (winter 1996): 635–47.

Olney, James. " 'I Was Born': Slave Narratives, Their Status as Autobiography and as Literature." In *The Slave's Narrative*, edited by Charles T. Davis and Henry Louis Gates, Jr., 148–74. New York: Oxford University Press, 1985.

Pelton, Robert D. *The Trickster in West Africa*. Berkeley and Los Angeles: University of California Press, 1980.

Pryse, Marjorie. "Introduction: Zora Neale Hurston, Alice Walker, and the 'Ancient Power' of the Black Woman." In *Conjuring: Black Women, Fiction, and Literary Tradition*, edited by Marjorie Pryse and Hortense Spillers, 1–24. Bloomington: Indiana University Press, 1985.

"Remembering Ralph Ellison" *American Visions* 9 (August/September 1994): 34–8.

Roberts, John. *From Trickster to Badman*. Philadelphia: University of Pennsylvania Press, 1989.

Rothberg, Michael. " 'We Were Talking Jewish': Art Spiegelman's *Maus* as 'Holocaust' Production." *Contemporary Literature* 35.4 (winter 1994): 661–87.

Ross, Nancy Wilson. *Three Ways of Asian Wisdom*. New York: Simon & Schuster, 1966.

Rushdy, Ashraf H. A. "The Phenomenology of the Allmuseri: Charles Johnson and the Subject of the Narrative of Slavery." *African American Review* 26 (fall 1992): 373–94.

Shelley, Percy Bysshe. *A Defense of Poetry*, edited by Albert S. Cook. Boston: Ginn & Company, 1890.

Stevens, Wallace. "The Idea of Order at Key West." In *Modern Poems*, edited by Richard Ellmann and Robert O'Clair, 96–98. New York: W. W. Norton & Company, 1973.

Suzuki, Daisetz Teitaro. *Manual of Zen Buddhism*. New York: Grove Press, 1960.

———. *The Zen Doctrine of No Mind*. London: Rider, 1969.

Tolstoy, Leo. *What Is Art?* Indianapolis: Bobbs-Merrill, 1982.

Wall, Cheryl. "Introduction: Taking Positions and Changing Words." In *Changing Our Own Words,* edited by Cheryl Wall, 1–15. New Brunswick, N. J.: Rutgers University Press, 1991.

West, Cornel. *Keeping Faith*. New York: Routledge, 1993.

Whitten, Norman E., Jr. "Contemporary Patterns of Malign Occultism among Negroes in North Carolina." In *Mother Wit from the Laughing Barrel,* edited by Alan Dundes, 402–18. New York: Garland Publishing, 1981.

Wright, Richard. "Blueprint for Negro Writing." In *Richard Wright Reader,* edited by Ellen Wright and Michel Fabre, 35–49. New York: Harper & Row, 1978.

———. "How 'Bigger' Was Born." In *Native Son*. New York: Harper & Row, 1940.

———. "The Literature of the Negro in the United States." In *White Man Listen!* Garden City, N. Y.: Doubleday & Company, 1957.

———. *Native Son*. New York: Harper & Row, 1940.

———. "Twelve Million Black Voices." In *Richard Wright Reader,* edited by Ellen Wright and Michel Fabre, 144–241. New York: Harper & Row, 1978.

Index

Permissions

Grateful acknowledgement is made for permission to reprint materials from the following sources:

Chapter 1 first appeared as "From the Comic Book to the Comic: Charles Johnson's Variations on Creative Expression" in *African American Review* 30:4 (winter 1996). Reprinted by permission of the publisher.

Excerpt from Charles Johnson's letter to John Gardner dated October 29, 1974, published by permission of Charles Johnson via Georges Borchardt, Inc.

Excerpt from Charles Johnson's letter dated December 3, 1974, published by permission of Charles Johnson via Georges Borchardt, Inc.

Excerpts from *Faith and the Good Thing* by Charles Johnson published by permission of Charles Johnson, via Georges Borchardt, Inc.

Cartoons reproduced from *Black Humor* and *Half-Past Nation Time* by Charles Johnson published by permission of Charles Johnson, via Georges Borchardt, Inc.

Excerpts from *Oxherding Tale* by Charles Johnson published by permission of Indiana University Press.

Excerpts from *Being and Race* by Charles Johnson published by permission of Indiana University Press.

Excerpts from *The Sorcerer's Apprentice* by Charles Johnson published with the permission of Scribner, a Division of Simon and Schuster. Copyright © 1986 Charles Johnson.

Excerpts from *Middle Passage* by Charles Johnson published with the permission of Scribner, a Division of Simon and Schuster. Copyright © 1989 Charles Johnson.

About the Author

Jonathan Little is Associate Professor of English at
Alverno College in Milwaukee, Wisconsin.